British Society for International Understanding

BRITISH SURVEY HANDBOOKS

General Editor: JOHN EPPSTEIN

III

GREECE

BRITISH SURVEY HANDBOOKS

GREECE

Compiled by
KATHLEEN GIBBERD

CAMBRIDGE
AT THE UNIVERSITY PRESS
1944

CAMBRIDGE
UNIVERSITY PRESS

University Printing House, Cambridge CB2 8BS, United Kingdom

Cambridge University Press is part of the University of Cambridge.

It furthers the University's mission by disseminating knowledge in the pursuit of education, learning and research at the highest international levels of excellence.

www.cambridge.org
Information on this title: www.cambridge.org/9781107426146

© Cambridge University Press 1944

First published 1944
First paperback edition 2014

A catalogue record for this publication is available from the British Library

ISBN 978-1-107-42614-6 Paperback

Additional resources for this publication at www.cambridge.org/9781107426146

CONTENTS

MAP

available for download from www.cambridge.org/9781107426146

EDITORIAL NOTE

This handbook has been brought up-to-date at the time of going to press, but like other books in the same series it does not attempt to describe the last phases of the changing military situation. Its object is rather to provide an accurate background by showing the constant factors in the life of the Greeks, the traditions and ideas which are in their minds, and the known consequences of the enemy occupation from which they have suffered. We are greatly indebted to members of the Greek Department of Information for contributions of fact, and to British officials for reading the typescript and suggesting improvements. The appendix is contributed by a British subject who has had long experience of work with the Greek Red Cross.

JOHN EPPSTEIN

September 1944

GREECE

═══

CHAPTER I

GEOGRAPHY OF GREECE

A line drawn diagonally across the map of Europe from north-west to south-east would join the two great island nations of Europe—Great Britain and Greece. But whereas Great Britain is entirely cut off by sea from the Continent, the greater part of modern Greece lies in the continental mainland and there has a common frontier with four other Balkan countries. Thus, Greece may be said to have one foot in south-eastern Europe and one in the Mediterranean, a position which partly accounts for a very different history from our own.

CONFIGURATION OF THE COUNTRY. The Greek mainland, excluding its southern extension, Morea —more commonly called by its old name, the Peloponnese—is roughly in the form of a crescent, embracing the waters of the northern Aegean and with its back to the Ionian Sea. Its long upper arm seems, on the map, to support the countries of Albania, Yugoslavia and Bulgaria, while reaching out to touch the western limit of Turkey. Under the curve of the arm, like an excrescence, is the curiously shaped peninsula of Chalcidike. Almost resting on the nether arm is the long island of Euboea. South of the crescent and separated from it by the Gulfs of

Corinth and Aegina is the Peloponnese, which, although linked to the mainland by the Isthmus of Corinth, was converted into a large island by the completion of the Corinth Canal in 1893. Farther south, by sixty miles of the Mediterranean, is Crete. These are the larger portions of Greek territory and they are set in a constellation of small islands—the Ionian islands, forming a chain down the west coast, and on the east the three hundred islands of the Greek Archipelago, scattered like irregular stepping-stones from Greece to Asia Minor.

The total area of the country, including all the islands, is estimated at 50,147 square miles, that is, a little more than half the size of Great Britain or approximately equal to England without Wales. The coast line is out of all proportion to this, for it is broken by innumerable creeks, peninsulas and bays. The sea, therefore, is the first geographical factor for this country, and second to it are the mountains. Almost the whole of Greece is mountainous. In the mainland the Pindus mountains form a backbone with ramifications over the whole area. The Peloponnesus mountains radiate from the central highlands of Arcadia. Crete has four mountain groups and the highest peaks hold the snow all the year round. Nearly all the smaller islands are dominated by hills or high rocks. The people of Greece live on the coastal plains, in wide, low valleys among the mountains and on high plateaux; but four-fifths of the land is unsuitable for cultivation, consisting of forest, scrub or bare rock. In these circumstances it is not surprising that the total population is less than that of Greater London. In 1938 it was estimated at 7,207,000. The only large towns, by western standards, are Athens, with its port Piraeus (1,125,000), and Salonica (575,000).

This sketch of the position and main physical features of the country is the necessary preliminary to a more detailed examination of its geography. For this purpose it will be convenient to follow five natural divisions: Southern Greece (the Peloponnese); Central Greece; Northern Greece (Thessaly and Epirus); North-eastern Greece (Macedonia and western Thrace); Crete and the smaller islands.

THE PELOPONNESE. Like other parts of Greece, the Peloponnese has a very indented coastline, but economically the coast is not here so closely related to the interior of the country as it is farther north. In parts it is steep and inhospitable and except on the channel in the north such ports as exist are not easily accessible from the lowland plains or upland plateaux, where most of the people live. Sparta, for instance, the ancient centre of civilization for this region, lies in a fertile plain not far distant from the Gulf of Laconia in the south, but a rocky ridge bars the way to the sea. Rivers in the Peloponnese, as elsewhere in Greece, are of little use for navigation. Owing to the prevailing limestone and to the mountainous nature of the country, they are, for the most part, rushing torrents which sometimes plunge into chasms and find an underground course to the sea. The limestone also produces lakes and swamps. These last, although unhealthy, are often extremely productive and are particularly suitable for the growth of maize (an alien crop imported from America) wherever the water drains away in full summer.

The centre of the Peloponnese is the great upland of Arcadia. Here at a distance of no more than some thirty miles from the sea, but barred from it by difficult country, the shepherd and goatherd live much as they did in classical times, although much less comfortably than in the idealized Arcadia of legend and literature. The weather is by no means always serene and when a storm breaks it may strew rocks and rubble over the lonely farmsteads.

One of the most genial and productive parts of the Peloponnese is the promontory of Messenia in the south. Here, besides the currant-grape, figs, oranges and dates are grown, mulberry trees are cultivated and there are the usual vineyards and olive groves. The north-west corner is, however, economically the most important for it is part of the great currant-producing region of Greece, a factor which did not exist in ancient times; the presence of Olympia in this corner shows that to the ancient Greeks this was neutral territory where Greek peoples from all quarters could meet in friendly rivalry. The largest town in the Peloponnese is the port of Patras, near the entrance to the Gulf of Corinth, and the export centre for the currant trade. Corinth, once a city commanding land and sea routes, has now a secondary importance.

CENTRAL GREECE. Central Greece may be considered as occupying the lower arm of the crescent which forms the mainland; it reaches northward to the southern limits of Thessaly. For modern Greece as for ancient Greece, this is the most important part of the country. Near the nether tip of the crescent is Athens and its port Piraeus, combining the political capital and the chief port of call for all sea-going traffic.

The Pindus mountains, which form a backbone in the Greek mainland, extend southward into this part of the country and almost at right angles to this main range there are lateral ranges stretching eastward. Between these lateral chains there is a series of low fertile plains reaching towards the sea and it is in these that the population is concentrated, as it was in ancient times. The most southerly plain is that of Attica, and here Athens is situated. Small hills, which break the plain, rise from behind and within the town, the most important being the Acropolis (literally, 'the upper part of the city'). This, which was once the fortress of ancient Athens, now dominates the city—a magnificent reminder of a bygone age. On its summit there stand the broken, but still beautiful, marble columns of the ancient temple, the Parthenon. This is the first sight in Athens which every traveller looks for, and the white marble, sometimes turned to pale gold by the sunlight, can be seen from miles away in the plain.

When Greece regained her independence in 1830, Athens was a mere village and the port of Piraeus a few fishermen's huts. In the next hundred years, both places first became typical Balkan towns, with donkeys and mule-carts plodding through dirty streets, and afterwards developed into characteristic cities of modern Europe. Piraeus is now like a smaller reproduction of Marseilles, and Athens presents in its main streets the usual features of a European capital city—modern shops, blocks of flats, trams, taxis and traffic lights.

The plain of Attica is separated from the plain of

Boetia by a range of mountains extending from Mt. Parnassus in the Pindus and including Mt. Helicon. In a narrow valley at the foot of Parnassus is the ancient town of Delphi, once sacred to the god Apollo and famous for its oracle, a shrine which was the symbol of such religious unity as there was between the Greek city States of classical times.

Wherever among the mountains there is water and cultivable land, there will be a village of white or pink-washed houses, clustering round a central square. All around are mountain slopes, some wooded with great plane trees, some terraced with steep vineyards or olive groves. Here and there are dark patches where the tobacco plant is grown, or lighter ones, showing a field of maize.

NORTHERN GREECE. Farther north are those regions of Greece which were not part of the State when Greece acquired her independence in 1830, but were 'redeemed' later. Northern Greece occupies the body of the crescent and lies between a line drawn westwards from the north coast of the island of Euboea to the Gulf of Arta and the boundaries of Albania and Greek Macedonia.

The Pindus range runs right through the centre of this region with the remote heights of Epirus on its western flank and the wide plains of Thessaly to the east. The general aspect of the country is different from Central Greece. There are fewer vineyards, olive groves and fig trees. Oak forests cover some of the mountain sides and on others the pine-woods make unbroken shadow. The sea is farther off and the means of travel is not by small coastal steamer or a sailing ship, but by motor bus or train (the main railway of Greece crosses Thessaly) where they avail; but, once off the beaten track, it is mostly a matter of foot-slogging by the side of a pack mule. The climate is less gentle; the skies are more often clouded and the air has lost the translucent quality of the air of Attica. In Epirus (the northern part of which was restored to Greece in 1912 after the first Balkan war) sheep-rearing is the main occupation of the people living in the mountains, but in the south, near the Gulf of Arta, there are upland plains where maize is grown. Most of the coast of Epirus is inhospitable, with few harbours. On the other side of the Pindus range the plains of Thessaly lie encircled by mountains and intersected by a rocky ridge. The River Peneios cuts through this ridge and finally finds its way to the sea through the serene valley of Tempe, with Mt. Olympus to the north and Mt. Ossa to the south. The Thessalonian plains are the chief corn-growing areas of Greece.

MACEDONIA AND GREEK THRACE. The long upper arm of the crescent of modern Greece consists of Macedonia and Thrace. Here is territory which has been much disputed and was only recently won back by Greece. Macedonia, a province twice the size of Wales, was almost unexplored at the beginning of this century, and the population was then a mixed one of Greeks, Turks, Slavs and Vlachs, with an established colony of Jews in the port of Salonika. It is a wild mountainous stretch of country running parallel to the sea, but sloping from the mountains in the west there are, in Central Macedonia, wide stretches of plain, particularly round Salonika. Formerly much of this flat land was marshy and malarial, but ambitious schemes of drainage and land reclamation were carried out in the 1920's in order to provide settlements for thousands of Greek refugees from Asia Minor. Before the present war there were extensive tobacco plantations, cotton plantations, silk farms and grain lands worked by the settlers. Moreover, by an exchange of populations between Greece and Bulgaria, and Greece and Turkey, the province had become almost entirely Greek in nationality. Salonika, at the mouth of the Vardar river, is not only the great outlet for all Macedonia, but for all the Balkan region beyond. It stands at the end of a series of valleys leading northward to Belgrade over the watershed by Skoplje, which has been one of the great highways of history. Down these valleys the Roman legions went from the Danube to the Aegean; up this route the Allies fought in the last European war; down it again swarmed the Germans in 1941. Important railways as well as roads converge upon Salonika.

A line going north from Salonika connects with the European railway system by way of Belgrade, and this is continued southwards through Larissa, the chief town of Thessaly, and on through Thermopylae to Athens—thence a line runs to Corinth to connect with the two railways of the Peloponnese—one following the coast west and south to Kyparissia and the other threading its way across the centre to meet this again at the terminus. Another leaves Salonika in a north-westerly direction for Monastir in Southern Yugoslavia and, still more important, is the line going east to Constantinople.

The peninsula of Chalcidike which thrusts into the sea like a trident from the plain of Salonika, is chiefly of interest on account of the religious communities which have been for centuries established in the region of Mt. Athos, in the most easterly of the three prongs. Here a number of monasteries and hermitages form an almost independent republic. The 5000 monks of the Orthodox Church come from other countries besides Greece; they support themselves on their own lands and maintain a mediaeval way of life.

Eastwards from Salonika and beyond a mountain ridge is the plain of Seres, watered by the River Struma, and beyond this again is the valley of the Drama with the port of Kavalla facing Thasos, a small wooded island. This port has been much coveted by Bulgaria. Eastwards again is the valley of the River Nestos usually considered as marking the boundary between Macedonia and Thrace. The rest of the region, Greek or Western Thrace, is mostly lowland and at the outbreak of the present war was fairly densely populated, largely by refugee settlements. It has an outlet to the sea at Dedeagach (Alexandropolis) which was for a short period Bulgarian (1912–18).[1] It is situated a few miles from the main stream of the River Maritsa which forms the frontier between Greece and Turkey.

This north-eastern part of Greece has always been extremely vulnerable to attack from the north. Elsewhere Greece has a sea frontier, but here there is no natural boundary and the valleys have always provided relatively easy means of invasion.

[1] It was one of the grievances of the Bulgarians before the present war that they did not secure possession of this part to which they held they were entitled by the provision of the Treaty of Neuilly assuring them access to the Aegean.

THE GREEK ISLANDS. The Greek islands may be considered in three divisions—the Ionian islands of the west coast; the Aegean islands, including the Northern Sporades and Cyclades; and Crete.

The Ionian islands were handed over to Greece by Great Britain in 1864. Among others they include Corfu, Leukas (Santa Maura), Cephalonia, Ithaka and Zante. The last three, together with neighbouring parts of the mainland constitute the main currant-producing area of the world. As will be seen later, it is on the successful cultivation and export of this 'luxury product' that the economic life of modern Greece has until recently largely depended.

Nearly all the islands of the Aegean Sea except the Dodecanese are Greek territory. In the north the Northern Sporades, lying chiefly near the large island of Euboea, are continued in Samothrace and Lemnos to the entrance to the Dardanelles. A few small islands including Imbros and Tenedos near this strategic passage have been retained by Turkey.

In the south the Cyclades extend from the seas neighbouring Piraeus, whence the nearest isles can be seen like sails on the horizon, right across to the shores of Asia Minor. Mitelene, Chios and Samos are close to these shores. The south-eastern group of islands in the South Aegean constitute the Dodecanese, of which the largest, Rhodes, is of great historic interest and strategic importance. Despite Greek claims based on the nationality of the inhabitants, this archipelago has been retained by Italy since the Italian fleet seized them from Turkey in 1912–13 (see p. 30).

None of the Aegean islands can be considered self-supporting—some in fact are little more than

rocks rising from the sea with a little strip of cultivation bordering the shores. Most of them produce
wine, olive-oil and fruits and perhaps a little grain.
Herds of goats give a milk supply. The inhabitants,
peasants, fishermen and sailors, live in white-
washed, cube-shaped houses which in many places
climb steeply up the hill side. In normal times there
is a coastal traffic of sailing ships or caiques, and
motor boats or benzinas, plying between the islands
and the mainland; but larger vessels also pass
through the archipelago, and these call at Syros, a
port in the island of that name and a recognized halt
between Greece and the Levant. Contrary to a
popular notion the Aegean is by no means usually
blue or calm; terrific storms blow up very quickly,
forcing ships that are due to sail to stay in harbour
and threatening with destruction the fishing boats
that have to get home past dangerous rocks.

Crete, the southernmost part of Europe, lies
60 miles from the southern tip of the Peloponnese
and 110 miles from the nearest point in Asia Minor.
It is about one-third the size of Sicily and equally
mountainous. For the most part the coast rises
steeply from the sea. Among the mountains there
are deep ravines, some so narrow that the daylight
never penetrates. There are also large caves. The
highest mountains are never free of snow and the
general aspect is of wild ruggedness and splendour.
But there are regions where rocks, ravines and pine
forests give place to upland plains, such as the Omalo
in the White Mountains. Here in the summer
months there are good, wide grazing grounds.
Although nowadays there are few towns of importance—Heraklion and Canea are the chief—in the

Homeric age there were over three hundred flourishing cities. The island was, in fact, the centre of the Great Minoan civilization, a civilization which archaeologists were still reconstructing when interrupted by the invasion by Germany in the summer of 1941.

Chapter II

OUTLINE OF HISTORY

(FROM CLASSICAL TIMES TO THE END OF THE BALKAN WARS)

IMPORTANCE OF THE CLASSICAL TRADITION. The classical culture of Greece, which reached its highest point in literature, architecture, sculpture, philosophy and in the foundation of democracy in the fifth and fourth centuries B.C. (480–338 B.C.), gives to the Greeks of to-day an historic sense far more vital than that which Mussolini sought to revive in the Italians, by his unburying of Imperial memories. Few Italians other than the churchmen can speak Latin. But the Greek of the great playwrights, Aeschylus, Sophocles and Euripides, perpetuated in the street-names of modern Athens, is read without difficulty in the secondary schools of modern Greece. Homer, even, is far more intelligible to them than Chaucer to the young Englishman, and every educated person can read the New Testament in its original Greek. It is true that there has been a deliberate revival of classical Greek as a national policy. But despite the incorporation of every modern and scientific term in the current language,[1] its structure and idiom is sub-

---

[1] E.g. from an article on the 26th Anniversary of the R.A.F., *Hellas*, 7 April 1944:

Ἡ Βρεττανικὴ ἀεροπορία ἐπανηγύρισε ἀφ' ἑαυτῆς τὴν ἐπέτειόν της, ὑψώσασα τὴν δρᾶσίν της εἰς θεώρατα ὕφη. Ἀνεξαρτήτως τῶν ἐπιχειρήσεων νεωτέρας καὶ ὅμως ἀπείρως ἰσχυρᾶς ἀεροπορικῆς δυνάμεως, τῆς Ἀμερικανικῆς, 8000 Βρεττανικὰ νυκτερινὰ βομβαρδιστικὰ ἔρριψαν τον Μάρτιον 28000 τόννους βομβῶν

stantially the same as it was in the age of Pericles.
It is this continuity of language which, despite the
admixture of many races in the Greek mainland and
among the Greek-speaking populations of the
Middle East, has made Greek nationality a genuine
thing.

THE BYZANTINE LEGACY. While the memory of
classical Hellas, enshrined in language and literature, and recalled by the ruins of temples and
statuary, gives the Greeks the sense that theirs is one
of the great mother countries of human civilization,
it is largely the Byzantine Empire which holds the
place of honour in their history books. The lightning
conquests of Alexander of Macedon, who as 'leader
of the Greeks' had in thirteen years (336–323 B.C.)
subdued Babylon and sown the seeds of Hellenic
culture in all the countries bordering upon the
eastern Mediterranean, are regarded as the prelude
to that Hellenic conquest of the Roman conquerors
of Greece. In a remarkably short time even the laws
of the eastern half of the Roman Empire were promulgated in Greek. The division of the Empire into
a Western and an Eastern domain, A.D. 325, within
a generation of the conversion of Constantine to

ἐναντίον ἐχθρικῶν στόχων καὶ τὸ μεγαλύτερον μέρος τῶν βομβῶν
τούτων ἐρρίφθη ἐπὶ γερμανικοῦ ἐδάφους.

'The Royal Air Force celebrated its anniversary by
reaching new heights in its activities. Without including
the operations of a new, still immensely powerful air
force, the American, which have been on an increasingly
large scale, 8000 British night bombers dropped during
the month of March 28,000 tons of bombs on enemy
targets, the greater part of the tonnage falling on German
territory.'

Christianity, led to a progressive differentiation of culture, customs and religious thought between East and West. So soon as the Empire of the East became entirely separate from the Empire of Latin Europe, it had become essentially a Greek dominion; and its centre, Constantinople—the new capital built by Constantine upon the site of Byzantium—was called 'the new Rome' and believed to inherit all those claims to the leadership of the world which had belonged to the ancient capital of the Roman Empire. The Byzantine Empire was essentially theocratic; Church and State, the Imperial office and the Episcopate were closely interlocked. In consequence, when in A.D. 1053 the final ecclesiastical separation from the Papacy followed the political division of the Empire, the Greek or, as it came to be called, Orthodox Church combined with the Greek framework of political society and the Greek ascendency in trade and shipping to form the ideas of many millions of people in Eastern Europe, in Egypt, in the Mediterranean and upon the western fringes of Asia.

THE IMPERIAL SENSE. The story of the Byzantine Empire is a long, complex and much-neglected chapter in European history. It had its major triumphs, particularly in the days of Justinian (A.D. 482–565) and his successor Heracleisos, whose armies not only reconquered Southern Italy and Sicily but occupied Tunisia as well. It had its trials —attacks by the Avars and the Persians on the one side, and by the Bulgars on the other—and its defeats—the weakening effect of the Latin Crusades and the final collapse before the onslaught of the

Turks. It is from this ultimate defeat that begins the history of modern Greece of which this chapter treats. But it would be a profound mistake to regard the fall of Constantinople as the end of the great Byzantine tradition. It is still vigorous in each of the Orthodox Churches into which the Eastern Church has been divided as the consequence of that very nationalism which regained Greece her freedom. So much of the civil as well as ecclesiastical government, so much of the commerce and finance of the Ottoman Empire remained in Greek hands, that in a sense it is true to regard the Ottoman Empire, despite its tyranny and corruption, as the successor rather than the destroyer of the empire of Byzantium. Hence it is that the Greeks have, as well as their pride in their classical past, and as well as their attachment to the Orthodox Church, a certain imperial tradition. The role of a small nation does not sit easily upon them. It has before now been the cause of inconvenient ambitions, of which the unhappy campaign in Asia Minor in 1918–22 is one example and the Greek aspirations to Northern Epirus another. Suffice it to say that when a Greek thinks of Hellas or of Hellenic civilization his conception of it is by no means confined to the Greek state of to-day: he is equally conscious of the Greeks of the Dodecanese, of the eastern Mediterranean coasts, Cyprus and Alexandria, and of his fellow-countrymen sailing the seven seas.

TURKISH RULE. The capture of Constantinople by the Turks in 1453 is indeed one of the great turning-points of European history; but it must not be allowed to obscure the fact that Constantinople, renamed Istanbul, remained throughout the Ottoman Empire a predominantly Greek city and that a great deal of the administration, as well as all the trade of the Empire, was continued by the Greeks under their new rulers, the Patriarchate and the Greek clergy being retained by the Turks as a convenient mechanism of government. Soon after the fall of Constantinople, the whole of Greece itself came under Turkish rule. Macedonia and Thessaly had been conquered more than half a century earlier, and so had parts of what is now Central Greece. Apart from these Turkish invasions, some Greek territories had fallen into the hands of Frankish adventurers and suffered servitude and misrule from them until they too were occupied by the Turks.

For four hundred and fifty years the territories which now form Greece and the Balkan countries were provinces of the Ottoman, or Turkish Empire. The only interruption was the transitory and limited success of the Venetians who bombarded Athens in 1687, partially destroying the Parthenon, and a few years later acquired the Peloponnese. The Turks, however, retook this peninsula in 1715.

Like other subject nations of the Turk the Greeks had to submit to local Turkish overlords, pay the special taxes levied on non-Moslems and provide each year a quota of young boys, 'the Janissaries', to be trained as the Sultan's bodyguard and converted to the Moslem faith.

But like other religious communities within the Ottoman Empire the Greeks formed a *millet* or self-governing entity as far as their internal affairs were concerned. The head of this *Millet-i-Rum* (the community of all the Orthodox Christians) was the

Greek Patriarch who lived in Constantinople. Until Orthodox Christians in other Balkan countries formed their own branches of the Orthodox Church the Patriarch was the recognized head of all Orthodox Christians in the Empire, and the fact that he was always a Greek gave the Greek people a superior status as compared with other Balkan subjects. In the Greek villages the parish priests both attended to the spiritual needs of the people and, assisted by village notables, presided over a simple court held on the Church premises. Here ordinary disputes between members of the Christian community were settled, while more complicated matters involving, for example, questions of inheritance, were referred to the Patriarchate. It will be readily understood how these Church arrangements helped to keep alive among ordinary Greeks a consciousness of their nationality and memories of past greatness.

Towards the end of the seventeenth century the Turkish Empire showed signs of decline and the position of the Christian population improved. The Central Turkish Government lost some of its control of outlying territories and became more ready to make gestures of good will to its Christian subjects. The personal service of Greek peasant to Turkish overlord was commuted to a money payment, and in many districts the peasants became virtually the free owners of small holdings. In the towns the intellectual ability of the Greeks found more scope than formerly. Greek officials were increasingly employed by the Turkish Government in positions of responsibility, notably in Bulgaria in the eighteenth century. They were known as Phanariots from the quarter of Constantinople in which the

Patriarchate is situated. But culturally they remained essentially Greek, and did not adopt either the language or religion of the Turks.

In commerce the Greeks had all along benefited by the contempt in which the Turks held the merchant's calling. They eventually carried on most of the trade of the Ottoman Empire, and by the end of the eighteenth century there were Greek merchant houses in various cities of Europe. These commercial outposts were a means of interesting European countries in the aspirations of subject Greece and, when the struggle for independence began, Greek merchant princes all over the continent contributed generously to the nation's cause.

THE WAR OF INDEPENDENCE. Greek Independence Day is observed on 25 March (since the Greek adoption of the Western Calendar in 1923), for on that day in 1821 the Archbishop of Patras unfurled the national flag and proclaimed the revolution in the Peloponnese. The way had been prepared by events in Europe as well as by the decline in Turkish authority. The French Revolution had been a clarion call throughout Europe to all who were chafing under oppression. Russia, whose sympathies with Greece were very strong, since the Orthodox Church was also the Church of Russia, had for a long time showed that she would be in favour of an independent Greece. As far back as 1770 a revolt had broken out in the Peloponnese under direct Russian encouragement and with a Russian fleet in the offing. It had been ruthlessly suppressed, chiefly by Albanian troops in the service of the Turks. The Albanian forces had remained as a continuing terror to the population and sharpened the determination for freedom. Britain and France, the two great Western Powers, had also become increasingly sympathetic towards the Greek cause, and there was reason to hope that they would lend the weight of their influence for the establishment of an independent Greek state.

At first there was no official intervention in the war by any of the Powers; but the cause of freedom, the great courage shown by the Greeks in their rebellion, and romantic sentiment for a country in which Western civilization had been born, brought many volunteers to help in the war. They included distinguished names. In 1824 Byron died on Greek soil, and has ever since been held in high honour by the Greeks. Early in 1827 Sir Richard Church and Lord Cochrane took over the commands of the Greek army and navy.

The struggle went in favour of the Greeks at first, chiefly because the Turks were at a disadvantage on the seas. From their island bases the Greeks sent fire ships against the Turkish fleet. Savage fighting and atrocities occurred on both sides. The Turks massacred the Greeks of Constantinople and publicly hanged the Patriarch on Easter Day. Greeks were also massacred in Macedonia and Thrace, and the incensed Greeks retaliated on any Turks who were living in Greece. At the end of 1824 Mahomet Ali, Pasha of Egypt, a vassal of the Turkish Sultan who had succeeded in making Egypt virtually independent, decided to come in on the side of Turkey. He invaded the Peloponnese with a well-trained army at a time when dissensions were weakening Greek resistance. This situation finally brought about the intervention of the interested Powers. A Triple Alliance between Russia, Great Britain and France was formed in 1827 and these Powers, calling for an armistice, undertook to mediate between Turkey and Greece. Before the Egyptian and Turkish forces withdrew, however, the Turkish navy was defeated in an engagement with the Allied Fleet, a French army threatened to invade the Peloponnese, and the Greeks inflicted a decisive defeat on a Turkish force near Thebes. The Peace of Adrianople concluded the war and the Russians, who had in the meantime gone to war with Turkey on their own account, exacted from Turkey a recognition of Greek independence.

At the Conference of London, the Triple Alliance gave formal recognition to the new State and settled its territories. These were eventually determined to include what is now Central Greece (with a northern frontier from the Gulf of Arta to the Gulf of Volo) the Peloponnese, and the islands of the Cyclades and Northern Sporades. The three Powers, Russia, Britain and France, thenceforward became the Protecting Powers of the new kingdom and declared that 'the Greek question is irrevocably settled'— but since the majority of the Greeks were still left as subject peoples, it is not surprising that later history disproved this statement. Thessaly, Epirus, Macedonia, Thrace, Crete, the Ionian and other islands still waited to be 'redeemed'.

THE NEW GREEK KINGDOM UNDER OTHO. The new Greek state, or rather its nucleus, began life under a president, but with the intention of finding a king. Prince Leopold of Saxe-Coburg (who later became

King of the Belgians) was first offered the throne, but he refused it. The problem was finally settled by the three Great Powers choosing Prince Otho of Bavaria, the son of an ardent devotee of Greek culture. The choice was partly dictated by political considerations. It was felt that the selection of a Bavarian prince was strictly neutral, since Germany could never have any pretext for interfering in Greek affairs.

Otho accepted the crown in 1832 at the age of seventeen, and the following year he arrived in the country of his adoption accompanied by an imposing host of Bavarian officials. Certain Bavarians formed a Council of Regency until he should come of age.

The first years of the new kingdom were not happy. The Bavarians ruled the country and, when Otho came of age, he showed no disposition to grant a constitution and was not sympathetic towards the people of Crete when they tried, unsuccessfully, to free themselves from the Turks. In 1843 the Greeks brought about a bloodless revolution, and Otho accepted their demands for the dismissal of the Bavarian officials and the establishment of a more democratic regime. In 1844 a National Assembly laid down a form of parliamentary government which Otho swore to accept.

This step forward, however, did not help Greece out of her troubles. Financial difficulties, party friction and brigandage produced unrest. Developments in Europe did not help. The Triple Alliance broke up and England and France fought on the side of Turkey and against Russia in the Crimean War. Greek sympathies were naturally with Russia, an Orthodox Power, and against Turkey, the traditional

enemy. Otho, who was now zealous for the extension of Greek territory, seized the occasion to try
to wrest Thessaly and Epirus from the Turks, but
he only succeeded in bringing the Anglo-French
fleet to Piraeus.

Otho's reign was in no way successful. Although
he was devoted to Greece to the end, he could never
bring himself to leave the government of the country
in the hands of his ministers. In 1862 he was forced
to abdicate.

A plebiscite of the people showed an overwhelm-
ing majority in favour of inviting an English prince
—Prince Alfred, second son of Queen Victoria—to
succeed to the throne. This, however, was ruled out
as the Three Powers had agreed in 1830 that no
member of their Royal families should accept the
Greek crown. The British Government, however,
undertook to find a substitute, and finally offered the
Greeks Prince George of Denmark (second son of
the future King Christian of Denmark). Prince
George's sister, Alexandra, had lately married the
heir to the British throne so that there was a strong
tie with Great Britain. Perhaps more important as
a sign of British goodwill was the cession of the
Ionian islands which had been occupied by Great
Britain in 1815.

GEORGE I, 'KING OF THE HELLENES'. Otho had been
proclaimed 'King of Greece' instead of 'King of the
Greeks', so as not to offend Turkey. Now that the
Greek state was established, however, this diplo-
matic caution was no longer necessary and King
George was declared to be 'King of the Hellenes'.
The ancient name of Hellas had long signified all

the lands which the Greeks held to be theirs by right. Most of these were still 'unredeemed' when George I came to the throne.

Immediately after his succession the new king accepted a revised Constitution (thought by some to be a model form of democratic government) and throughout his long reign of fifty years he remained a strictly constitutional monarch, exercising great tact through the storms of Greek politics. Two outstanding events of his reign were the emancipation of the other Balkan peoples and the unsuccessful attempt of the people of Crete to become united with independent Greece.

GREECE ACQUIRES THESSALY AND SOUTHERN EPIRUS. Greece had led the way of insurrection among Balkan countries and now others were feeling their way to freedom from the Turks. In 1878 Russia, after another war with Turkey, sought to establish by the Treaty of San Stefano a 'Greater Bulgaria' which would have been constructed at the expense of territories in Macedonia that the Greeks had always regarded as rightfully their own, although still in Turkish hands. The Congress of Berlin (June 1878), under the chairmanship of Bismarck, afterwards nullified this treaty. Meeting on what was still considered 'neutral ground' the Powers settled Balkan affairs, but without admitting Balkan delegates to the discussions. They recognized the independence of Serbia, Rumania and Montenegro, and left the adjustment of the northern frontier of Greece to be settled between Greece and Turkey. In 1881 this was drawn from a little north of the Vale of Tempe to Arta on the Ambracian Gulf. Greece thus acquired the Arta district of Epirus and the rich grain lands of Thessaly.

CRETE PREVENTED FROM UNION WITH GREECE. Meanwhile the people of Crete had been struggling for freedom and gaining nothing but paper promises from Turkey. The Congress of Berlin had left Crete in Turkish hands and the Turks would only yield it to Greece in exchange for Thessaly—and this Greece would not accept. There was constant bloodshed between the Moslems and the Christian population on the island. Early in 1897 Greek troops from the mainland landed in Crete for the express purpose of carrying out its annexation. The Powers thereupon intervened and an international force of British, French, Russian, Italian, German and Austrian troops occupied the island. (Germany and Austria later withdrew their forces, since these countries were not vitally interested.) The occupation lasted over a year, but it ended in the despatch of the last of the Turkish soldiers from Crete. The island was given self-government under Prince George of Greece as High Commissioner. It had its own flag and coinage, but was not united to Greece. In fact the Turks still held nominal sovereignty. Separation from the mother country was prolonged until the end of the first Balkan war in 1913.

FAILURE TO EXTEND NORTHERN FRONTIERS. At the same time the national desire to bring the other 'unredeemed' territories into the Greek kingdom had led to Greek irregulars crossing into Macedonia and over the frontier of Epirus. Turkey

immediately declared war, and bitter fighting followed in both provinces. The Greeks had neither
the money nor the military strength to take the
territories which they felt to be theirs, whereas the
Turkish army had been reorganized under a German
military mission. The Greeks were hopelessly defeated and nearly lost Thessaly. The Powers intervened to save the situation. An International
Financial Commission was established in Athens to
guarantee the payment of an indemnity to Turkey
and to see that the interest on foreign loans was also
paid.

One of the results of the defeat and humiliation
of Greece was to encourage Bulgarian aspirations in
Macedonia. This wild and mountainous province
had a mixed population of Greeks, Turks, Serbs,
Bulgarians, Vlachs, Jews and Albanians. In earlier
days, when all the Balkans were under Turkish rule,
the predominant culture of Macedonians had been
Greek, and all the Christians were to some extent
drawn together under the Greek Patriarch. This
religious bond, such as it was, however, had been
broken a generation before when, in 1870, the Turks,
acting on the divide-and-rule principle, had established a separate Church for the Bulgarians (the
Bulgarian Exarchate) as a rival to the Greek
Patriarchate. The Patriarch excommunicated the
Exarch and his clergy as schismatic, and from then
onwards there was intense rivalry between Patri-
archists and Exarchists, both of whom spread their
rival propaganda in Macedonia, which became a hot-
bed of trouble and unrest. Greeks and Bulgarians
were continually coming into conflict, and both
fought against the underpaid and ill-fed Turkish

soldiers who plundered indiscriminately. The Powers tried to intervene, but with little success. Finally chaos came to an end as the result of the revolutionary movement of the Young Turks, under their 'Committee of Union and Progress'.

The revolutionaries consisted partly of exiled Turks and partly of adventurers of varying nationality. Mustapha Kemal, the future ruler of Turkey, was among them from early days. They organized a revolutionary army in Salonika (whence the movement started), demanded that the Sultan should call a parliament and threatened to march on Constantinople. With a prospect of sharing in representative government the warring nationalities in Macedonia became reconciled and when the Young Turks, as they came to be called, having got themselves in the saddle, began to be even more oppressive than the former Turkish Government, the way was paved for an alliance against the common enemy.

ELEUTHERIOS VENIZELOS. By the end of 1919 Greece, although it had made considerable progress under King George I, was on the verge of chaos and revolution. The renewed demands of Crete for union with Greece had received no sympathetic response from the mother country where the Government was afraid of offending both the Protecting Powers and Turkey. This and the inefficiency of the Greek army were among the grievances which provoked a mutiny among some of the younger army officers. Premier had followed premier, and the rebellious officers, known as the Military League, began to dictate to the Greek parliament. It was at this juncture that M. Venizelos, destined to become one of

the most famous men of his time, was summoned
from Crete by the Military League to advise them;
at the end of 1910 he became Prime Minister.
Eleutherios Venizelos was then forty-four. He was
the descendent of a family of the Greek mainland
and, although born in Crete, had received his school
and university education in Greece. When Crete received her autonomy he became prominent as an
able statesman and had been a leader in the Cretan
movement for Union with Greece.

When he came to Athens, however, it was not to
effect this union but to put the mother country in
order. In this he had not only the King, but the
whole country behind him. In four years he brought
about a condition of security for life and property
that had not yet been known and the authority of
government and parliament was, for the time being
at least, established. The condition of the poorer
people was improved, the army and navy reformed,
and the administration freed from corruption. With
these successes behind him he was able to rid all
Greek territory of Turkish rule. At this time Turkey
was preoccupied with a war against Italy in Libya
and under her weakening authority all the Balkan
States were straining for freedom. It was a superb
opportunity for the burial of mutual antagonisms—
so long fostered by Turkey—and for a united front
against the common enemy. The fact that the
Powers were backing Turkey in her unsuccessful
attempt to keep order in the Balkans gave a final
incentive to the Balkan countries to co-operate. As
the result of the energy and diplomacy of M. Venizelos the Balkan League was formed. In 1912 the
Serbs, Bulgarians and Greeks were fighting together

against the Turks in what came to be known as the First Balkan War.

THE FIRST AND SECOND BALKAN WARS. The Balkan allies won a succession of victories on land and the Greeks, as well as sharing in these, put their navy to good service by guarding the Dardanelles and the Aegean, thus preventing the Turks from sending reinforcements by sea. Perhaps the most satisfactory victory for the Greeks was the capture of Salonika, which surrendered to a Greek army a few hours before a Bulgarian army arrived on the scene —a situation which caused some bitterness in Bulgaria, since the port was considered to be one of Bulgaria's legitimate claims. There was also tension between Bulgaria and Serbia, but the solidarity between the allies was sufficient to achieve complete victory. By the Treaty of London (30 May 1913), Turkey ceded to the Balkan League all territory beyond a line drawn from Enos on the Aegean to Media on the Black Sea, except Albania which the Powers insisted should be an independent state.

It then remained to share the spoils, and it was the attempt of Bulgaria to extend the territories at the expense of her former allies which led to the Second Balkan war. Greece and Serbia, firmly bound by a new Treaty of Mutual Assistance, resisted her and Rumania supported them. The second war lasted only a month and ended in the defeat of Bulgaria; but Turkey had taken advantage of the situation to recapture Adrianople.

GREEK TERRITORY DOUBLED. As the result of the two Balkan wars, Greece nearly doubled her terri-

tory and brought under the Greek Crown most of
the Greek peoples. The new gains included the rest
of Epirus, except the north, Macedonia, Crete and
some Aegean islands. There were still, however,
large numbers of Greeks in Turkish Thrace and in
Asia Minor, and these at first suffered much ill-
treatment from the Turks until M. Venizelos made
a firm protest backed by a threat of war.

Northern Epirus, or Southern Albania, was disputed territory. Under the Turks the whole of
Epirus had been one administrative region and
virtually self-governing, the clergy and local administration being mainly Greek. Now the population was a mixture of Moslem Albanians and Orthodox Albanians and Greeks; and the Italian Government, wishing to see a strong Albania, strongly urged
that it should form part of that small country.
A Commission sent to investigate on the spot made
the same recommendation. However, an insurrection broke out and the rebels set up their own
government. As a result of this the Powers compro-
mised by deciding that Northern Epirus should be
an autonomous province under Albanian rule.

Italy also stood in the way of the redemption of
other Greek territory in the Dodecanese. These
islands, lying off the west coast of Asia Minor, had
been occupied by the Italian fleet during the war
between Turkey and Italy in North Africa, and it
was understood that the occupation was only for the
duration of that war. The Italians, however, have
never evacuated the islands, despite the petitions of
the people of whom some 87% are Greek.

Germany and Austria were also powers unfavourable to Greece. After the conclusion of the Balkan

wars, these two powers showed a readiness to support Turkey and to back Bulgaria in her ambition to gain Macedonia. M. Venizelos was told quite clearly by the German Chancellor in April 1914 that Greece could not count on help from Germany against Turkey.

In the meantime, King George I had been murdered—it is said, by a half-wit—after a reign of fifty years in which he had been an exemplary constitutional sovereign. He was succeeded by his son, who was a very different character. King Constantine had received a military education in Germany where he had, among other honours, been made an honorary field-marshal. He appears to have had a great admiration for the Kaiser, whose favourite sister he had married. He thought of himself as a 'war-lord', and there was some justification for this in that he had led the Greek forces in the recent victorious campaigns, although it should be noted that the Greek army itself had been largely trained by a French military mission and fought with French guns.

Chapter III

POLITICAL HISTORY, 1914–1944

THE FIRST GREAT WAR. It was not surprising, in view of circumstances already described, that when the European war broke out in 1914 the King of Greece felt in some sympathy with Germany. Private communications from the Kaiser tried to induce him to range Greece on Germany's side. This was an impossible step, since the country was at this stage united behind Venizelos and his Liberal Government in their assertion of benevolent neutrality, and their guarantee to stand by the pact to defend Serbia if Bulgaria should attack her. Nor can it be assumed that the King either desired or was prepared to recommend such an alignment even though he may have felt, like many others, that Germany's was likely to be the victorious side.

At first there was some likelihood that Greece, under the leadership of Venizelos, would come into the war on the Allies behalf, without waiting for a Bulgarian attack on Serbia. Early in 1915 the Allies promised as a reward for this that Greece should receive that part of Asia Minor in which there was a large Greek population. This proposal appealed to M. Venizelos, who thought it worth while trying to buy off Bulgaria with an outlet to the sea in Macedonia, his argument being that it was worth while sacrificing a relatively small number of Greeks in a Bulgarian 'corridor' in order to bring the two million Greeks in Asia Minor under the Greek flag. He also proposed to come to terms with Rumania.

However, these negotiations came to nothing, and Bulgaria presently accepted a large loan from the other side and threw in her lot with Germany.

When in February 1915 the Allied fleets made their first attack on the Dardanelles, Venizelos wished to send a Greek landing force to assist them, but this idea was strongly opposed by Colonel Metaxas (as he then was), and finally, after a reluctant consent, was refused by King Constantine. Venizelos then resigned and one of his political opponents was appointed premier. In June of the same year, elections were held and the country was divided between those who supported the King and those who supported Venizelos. Despite the German propaganda campaign which was being carried on in the country, and although the issue was presented by the opponents of Venizelos as one of peace or war, the Liberals gained a majority and Venizelos again became premier. In the next few months the personal and political quarrel between the King and Venizelos became acute. In September Bulgaria mobilized and M. Venizelos immediately asked the King to order Greek mobilization so that Greece could stand by her pledge to go to the aid of Serbia. The King was finally persuaded, but those who supported him against Venizelos wished the mobilization to be for defence only, since they declared Serbia unable to put into the field the force stipulated in the treaty. Venizelos's answer to this was to ask for Allied help—a request that was immediately granted. The King objected to this on the grounds that it would put an end to Greek neutrality. His objection came too late, however, for the Allies were resolved. Venizelos felt obliged to resign, but even while he was having his final interview with his sovereign, the Allied forces were approaching Salonika to effect a landing.

In the following eighteen months Greece lost all the dignity, unity and stability that had belonged to the country at the outbreak of war. After an unsuccessful attempt of the British Government to gain the help of King Constantine by the offer of the island of Cyprus—an offer which the King rejected —it became clear to the Allies that they could not count on the Greek King or his Government for support. On the contrary, there were intrigues with the enemy. The new Greek Government repudiated the treaty with Serbia, and the Bulgarians invaded that country as a preliminary to overrunning Macedonia. Their entry into Eastern Macedonia was facilitated by the surrender, without a fight, of Rupel Fort, the guardian of a vital pass. The result of this defection was that the Allies agreed that Northern Epirus (Southern Albania) should come under Italian control, although Greek forces had been allowed to occupy this district at the beginning of the war. Thus Greece lost a claim to a territory which had been long coveted.

The Allies made various demands on Greece and sent a force to the island of Salamis. The King continued to vacillate; the Government was increasingly at variance with the will of the people. Finally Venizelos decided that his only course was to retire to Crete, a liberal stronghold where the loss both of Greek territory and Greek prestige was bitterly resented, and proclaim a rebellion. Later he moved to Salonika and set up a revolutionary government there. The Allies were unwilling to recognize this at first as Venizelos, after failing to get the King's backing, took up a definitely anti-monarchist attitude. Eventually, however, a French admiral was sent to Athens on behalf of the Allies to enforce the abdication of the King. This was accomplished after an unpleasant encounter with Greek forces. Constantine's second son, Alexander, succeeded to the throne and Venizelos returned to Athens, where he proceeded to put the country in order. Colonel Metaxas and other military chiefs were banished to Corsica. Later Venizelos visited Paris and London and arranged for food and munitions of war to be supplied to Greece. It was thus only during the last months of the war that Greek troops fought side by side with the Allies, but having come in at last they immediately distinguished themselves and in September 1918, in company with French and Italian troops, they dealt a knock-out blow to the German and Bulgarian forces. Their 'brilliant aptitude for mountain warfare' drew the special praise of the French Commander-in-Chief.

THE PEACE SETTLEMENT. At the Peace Conference in Paris, M. Venizelos headed the Greek delegation and impressed everyone with his statesmanlike qualities. The settlement of Greek claims against Turkey was, however, postponed until August 1920, when the Treaty of Sèvres was signed. This treaty, had it not been later repudiated by Turkey, would have satisfied all Greek claims. The north-eastern frontier of the new Greece was to be drawn only twenty miles west of Constantinople. It brought the important town of Adrianople and the peninsula of Gallipoli into the Greek kingdom. Nearly all the

Aegean islands would have become Greek territory, the chief exception being the Dodecanese which were left in Italian hands. (A separate agreement between Italy and Greece gave these to Greece but, as has already been stated, the transfer has never yet taken place.) Most important of all, the Smyrna district and hinterland were to be handed over to Greek administration, although the nominal sovereignty of Turkey was allowed to remain. A parliament was to be elected by the inhabitants and if, in five years' time, this body demanded that Smyrna be incorporated into the Greek kingdom, then the union was to be allowed.

M. Venizelos returned to Athens to receive the thanks of his fellow countrymen for his successful pleading of the Greek claims. But during his long absence a strong faction had grown against him, especially among those who supported the exiled King Constantine. Others perhaps were tired of hearing the praises of the Prime Minister, and the whole country was weary of being in an almost continuous state of war or mobilization since 1912. The elections at the end of 1920 showed a reaction of feeling against the man who had for years been a national hero and M. Venizelos resigned and left the country. In the meantime King Alexander had died suddenly and a tide of feeling for the recall of Constantine set in. Against the will of the Powers, who refused to recognize him as king, Constantine returned to Athens. In the next fifteen months, he was to be involved in the greatest disaster that had befallen his country in the first hundred years of its independence.

The Turkish Government had now repudiated the

Treaty of Sèvres. Moreover, the leaders of the New Turkey, under Mustapha Kemal, adopted a threatening attitude towards the Greeks who lived in scattered villages throughout Asia Minor. The Greek administration in Smyrna and the small Greek occupying force which, with the blessing of the Allies, had been landed there during the Peace Conference, were also imperilled. The new Greek Government, therefore, decided to start an offensive against Turkey. They hoped, not only to save their fellow Greeks, but to capture Ankara, the new Turkish capital which Kemal had instituted in Asia Minor. They also cherished dreams of reaching Constantinople. Greek forces, with King Constantine swiftly following, landed in Smyrna.

THE SMYRNA EXPEDITION. Despite striking initial successes, the expedition was doomed. The Powers were unwilling to support it, the army was inadequately equipped and the officers owed their appointments to their royalist sympathies rather than to their experience in warfare. The Turks, whose strength and strategy had been underestimated, withdrew before the Greek advance until their enemies were within sixty miles of Ankara and then inflicted a terrible defeat upon them. King Constantine returned to Athens and his two chief ministers set off for European capitals to beg the assistance of the Great Powers. Italy, however, had long been jealous of the growing importance of the Greek kingdom and France was already on terms of friendship with Turkey, to whom she was supplying arms. The British Government refused to act without France and when eventually a conference was arranged in Paris the Turks made unacceptable demands. Shortly afterwards the Turks began a great counter-offensive, marched into Smyrna and in the few days following 9 September 1922 sacked and burned the Greek and Armenian quarters. Amid scenes of panic and horror the Greek population tried to escape by sea, and all who could find any kind of boat in which to leave the burning city made off to the islands and eventually to the mainland.

The immediate result was that a group of officers who had landed on the island of Chios formed a Revolutionary Committee, demanding the abdication of the King and the trial of the ministers responsible for the Smyrna expedition. King Constantine accepted the demand and died in exile a few months later. He was succeeded by George II, the present King. Six ministers were brought to trial and shot. As a result of this summary act, Great Britain broke off diplomatic relations with Greece.

THE TREATY OF LAUSANNE. It was not till the summer of 1923 that the situation between Greece and Turkey was settled by the Treaty of Lausanne. By this settlement Greece lost almost every new gain that had come to her by the abortive Treaty of Sèvres. Her Turkish frontier was fixed at the River Maritsa, so that Turkey got back Adrianople and Gallipoli. All Greek claims to territory in Asia Minor were abandoned.

The most acute problem following the rout in Asia Minor was the settlement of the thousands of refugees who made their way to the mainland, and this was followed by the necessity of dealing with still more Greeks pouring into the mother country when a Convention between Greece and Turkey for the exchange of their minority populations was carried out. According to the estimate of the chairman of the League of Nations Commission, which was finally entrusted with the task of re-establishment, 1,300,000 Greeks were uprooted from their Turkish homes and transported to Greece in exchange for about a tenth of that number of Turks. Under the auspices of the League of Nations a loan was raised to finance this tremendous enterprise of providing homes and work for the refugees, many of whom became producers of tobacco in Macedonia, but so large an addition to a population that was already poor was a great economic burden.

By force of circumstances, although under no official arrangement, there was also an exchange of minority populations between Greece and Bulgaria. When both these transfers of peoples were complete there were no longer any large Greek communities living outside Greek territory except in the Dodecanese and in the island of Cyprus. This island, where approximately four-fifths of the population were Greek and about one-fifth Turkish, had been occupied by the British in agreement with Turkey in 1878 and formally annexed in 1924. As has already been said, it was offered during the war to Greece on condition that she immediately joined the Allies. Since nearly all the 'unredeemed' Greeks had come back to Greece, it was natural that the quarter of a million Greek Cypriots should now wish to see the end of British rule, however beneficial that rule had been and, in 1931, there was a general uprising on the island. However, M. Venizelos, who was Prime Minister at the time, refused to back the rebels and the British restored order, imposed penalties and withdrew the measure of self-government which the Cypriots had hitherto enjoyed.

INTERNAL CONDITIONS FROM 1922 UNTIL METAXAS. From one point of view Greece appears to have been a very unsettled country during the eighteen years which separated the Smyrna disaster of 1922 from the next and the far greater catastrophe of the Axis invasion. The immediate effect of the Smyrna episode was the temporary government of Greece by a Revolutionary Committee. Partly because the King was held responsible for the Smyrna expedition, there was a strong feeling, especially among sections of the army and navy, for abolishing the monarchy in favour of a republican regime. In 1924 a Republic was duly formed, but excessive party strife continued and government followed government. M. Venizelos was recalled from his retirement to be premier once more in 1925 but resigned after one month. During the dissensions of the next four years there was a period of unsuccessful dictatorship under General Pangalos—it lasted only seven months, from January to August 1926. M. Venizelos came back for the last time in 1928 and held office for four years. There was an abortive *coup d'état* in 1933, when General Plastiras, who had led the military rebellion from the island of Chios after the rout from Smyrna, tried to alter by force the results of an election. But a much more serious affair occurred in 1935, when a military and naval insurrection broke out in protest against the royalist sympathies of the Government. Many officers who took part were afraid that the restoration of the monarchy would inevitably result in their losing their commands. However, the rising was put down and sentences passed on the ringleaders. General Plastiras had been the acknowledged leader of the insurgents although he had taken no active part, and M. Venizelos, who had been living in retirement in Crete, had placed himself at the head of the rebel units when they arrived in Suda Bay. Both were condemned to death in their absence. M. Venizelos died a natural death in Paris the following year after a life which, despite the mistakes fastened on by his enemies, was distinguished by the championship of Greek national aspirations and of democratic government. He was always an admirer of British institutions and in the councils of Europe he was recognized as one of the great statesmen of his day. He had been premier eight times and twice narrowly escaped death by assassination.

The chief result of the failure of the 1935 insurrection was to bring about the restoration of the monarchy, and towards the close of the year King George II left England to resume the Greek throne. In the next few months three of the chief party leaders died and since one of them was Prime Minister, his deputy, General Metaxas, became head of the Government. As a result of the preceding general election the two main groups of parties had almost exactly the same number of members, with the result that the fifteen Communist members held the balance.

However, the Communists never had the opportunity to profit by this situation, as parliament was first prorogued for five months and then General Metaxas persuaded the King to suspend those articles of the Constitution which dealt with the liberty of the subject and to proclaim martial law. He himself became Dictator. He justified this drastic action by reference to industrial disorders and a threatened general strike. From this moment until his death after the Italian invasion—that is, from August 1936 until January 1941—Metaxas held the country in an iron grip. Parliament was dissolved, the press rigidly censored, free trade unions were no longer allowed to function. In short, all the features of a democratic state were suspended, even to the expunging of the Funeral Oration of Pericles from the text books of the schools. There were also innovations on the German model, such as a secret police and uniformed organizations of a semi-military character.

To a people so politically minded as the Greeks these measures were abhorrent and, despite the outward semblance of order and the social reforms planned for the country's benefit by the Dictator, both Metaxas and the King, who had conferred the dictatorial powers, became the objects of popular hatred.

So much for the troubles and disturbances in Greece in the eighteen years before the Second Great War. But from another point of view there was much progress, particularly in the relations between Greece and her neighbours.

IMPROVED RELATIONS WITH TURKEY AND THE BALKANS. By a series of agreements Greece and Turkey turned enmity into friendship, and October 1930, eight years after the Smyrna tragedy, found M. Venizelos the honoured guest of the Turkish

Government in Ankara. The next year the Turkish premier paid a return visit and had an enthusiastic reception in Athens. Equally important was the growth of solidarity among the Balkan States. This was given outward form in the Balkan Pact of 1934, by which Greece, Turkey, Rumania and Yugoslavia 'guaranteed' the 'security of all the Balkan frontiers' and resolved on a policy of mutual consultation. Although Bulgaria, dissatisfied with these frontiers, remained out of this entente, she came to terms with the other Balkan States in 1938 when she signed a Treaty of Friendship and Non-Aggression. With Italy relations were not so promising, and they were to some extent embittered by the Italian refusal to give up the Dodecanese, but after the League of Nations had stood by Greece in 1923 and obliged the Italians to recall the troops which they had landed in Corfu, there was little apprehension in Greece as to the ambitions of Italy. The Italian invasion of Abyssinia was taken to mean that Italy was looking elsewhere than the Balkan countries for Fascist domination. When sanctions were called for by the League Greece, despite the cost to her trade, showed great readiness to cooperate. Later, when the Great Powers of the League weakened in carrying out sanctions to the full, there was naturally some uneasiness and eventually the Greek Government recognized the King of Italy as emperor of the newly acquired territory. With Germany there were growing economic agreements, and on Germany's side these were backed with much protestation of friendship.

In domestic affairs there was also gradual improvement. Under the Venizelos Government of

1928–32, the finances of the country embarked on a period of steady improvement which was unfortunately halted by the world economic crisis in 1931. With the help of foreign loans roads were built and a proper water supply provided for Athens. An agreement with the British Government gave Imperial Airways facilities in Greece and made Athens a port of call between Britain and the East. Various commercial agreements offered better prospects and although, when the economic crisis had been weathered, these were chiefly with Germany, this was because no other Power offered any alternative. The army and navy and civil police were also reorganized with British assistance.

The outbreak of war in September 1939 increased the feeling of solidarity among the Balkan peoples, but only temporarily; an atmosphere of *sauve-qui-peut* developed when German forces began to overrun the smaller countries of Europe and when France had yielded. While maintaining the strictest neutrality, Greece relied on help from Britain in the event of an assault on her territory. This had been promised her after the shock of the Italian occupation of Albania in the spring of 1939 and reaffirmed by Lord Halifax in the House of Lords in September 1940. Relations with Great Britain had been further strengthened by some generosity from Britain in the matter of the Greek external debt. This eased a burden which the Greeks had found exacting. Also Britain at long last (as the Greeks saw it) undertook to buy a great part of the Greek tobacco crop.

THE ITALIAN INVASION.   On 28 October 1940 the first invasion came. At 3 a.m. on that day General

Metaxas was handed an Italian ultimatum demanding the passage of Italian troops to 'certain strategic points'—it did not specify what these points were. The general, who had already expressed the feeling of the country in making a firm stand against Axis pressure was in no mind to yield and, even before the appointed time limit had run out, Italian troops were advancing over the Albanian frontier into Greece.

The immediate national response was to sink party differences in a single-minded enthusiasm for the defence of Greece. Patriotism was at white heat and the most bitter enemies of Metaxas rallied round him, as the national leader and symbol of defiance. When Metaxas died as a result of an operation in January 1941, he was succeeded in the premiership by M. Koryzis, the Governor of the National Bank, who retained his office until April, when he committed suicide in the face of the German conquest of his country.

In the meantime, as is well known, the Greeks after an initial withdrawal adopted the offensive and pursued the Italians into the Albanian mountains, fighting for six months with the utmost bravery and skill against the more numerous and more heavily armed, but retreating enemy. During this period Germany remained aloof from the conflict but an increasing number of German business men and 'tourists' poured into Greece and Bulgaria.

THE GERMAN INVASION.   With the spring of 1941, however, it became evident that Greece was now of strategic value to Germany as a base for operations in the Middle East. Yugoslavia was the main route

for this base and the two countries were invaded by
Germany simultaneously at the beginning of April.
Assisted by some 60,000 troops from Britain and the
Dominions, the Greeks continued their heroic resistance to the end, but the campaign against the
Germans was inevitably brief. On 15 April 1941 the
Germans were in Salonika and on the 27th they
entered Athens, whence the King and Government
had retired to Crete. The Cretan campaign followed
during the second half of May but the island was
quickly taken by German parachute troops. The
King and Government escaped with some difficulty
to Africa, and later to London, where they remained
until 1943 when both were established in Cairo.

In the meantime the Bulgarians had followed the
Germans and poured into Macedonia and Thrace.
This north-eastern part of Greece, with the exception of a small enclave around Salonika and the
province of Evros near the Turkish frontier was later
assigned by Germany to Bulgaria, and the Bulgarian
annexation was maintained with a ferocity that
stands out even against the general picture of occupied territories in the years 1941-4. The effects of
the occupation are dealt with in another chapter. It
is only necessary to add here a few details of political
developments.

GREEK RESISTANCE.   In spite of the most persistent
propaganda prior to the invasion and after it the
Germans have been singularly unsuccessful in win-
ning over the Greeks to collaboration. There has
been a puppet government in Athens under three
successive premiers—all of whom have been deprived of their Greek nationality by the King—and

they have tried to gain support for the Germans on the well-worn plea that the invaders intend to save Europe from Bolshevism. Other influential persons, who showed some readiness to cooperate at first, were said to have given up the attempt in disgust at the graft and corruption which were practised by Italian and German officials. Civil servants and other public officials who have remained at their posts have hampered the Germans by their lack of zeal in implementing regulations.

But all the time the war against the invader has never ceased, for thousands of Greeks fled to the mountains, where bands of guerillas have successfully held large areas of the country and unceasingly harassed the Germans, particularly in attacking their lines of communication. The largest guerilla band is the E.L.A.S. (National Popular Liberation Army). It is directed by a political organization, the E.A.M. (National Liberation Front), in which various parties have collaborated, but in which Communist influence has been predominant. It derived directly from the underground organization which opposed the Metaxist dictatorship before the war and had, therefore, a machinery of resistance which could be utilized and developed against the national enemy. The Communists—who were by no means the only opponents of the Metaxist regime—have been estimated by one source of information as 10% of the population; but the figure, if accurate, has no precise significance since most of those who call themselves Communist in Greece are not Communist in the strict meaning of the term, and in so far as they are peasants would not accept the principle of collective ownership. In a general way, therefore,

E.A.M. is probably best described as a 'left' organization which has not forgotten its hatred of the Metaxist regime and is inimical to the King, considering him as responsible for the setting up of the dictatorship. The chief rival to the E.A.M.—for despite the common enemy rivalry soon developed —was the E.D.E.S. (Free Democratic Greek Army), led by Colonel Zervas (later Colonel Zervas renamed his followers E.O.E.A.—National Bands of Greek Guerillas—and disclaimed any political ambitions). The third group, E.K.K.A., was led by Colonel Psaros until he was fatally attacked.

In the Greek mainland, where these groups of partisans and others have from time to time successfully attacked the German personnel and transport, E.L.A.S. has chiefly operated to the east of the Pindus Mountains and E.D.E.S. to the west. Unfortunately the feuds between these two bands, stimulated by the rumours which the Germans disseminated, led to civil war in the autumn of 1943. This was a bad time throughout Greece. The result of the Italian collapse was to turn the Greeks' most despised foe into a co-belligerent; the loss of Leros, Cos and Samos, so soon after the British landings had raised hopes of imminent liberation, was a bitter disappointment; and the food situation had deteriorated—partly because, in a mistaken optimism, some reserves of food had been used up.

After appeals for unity from the King and Government in Cairo, and from G.H.Q. Middle East, the civil strife between the guerillas was halted by an armistice in February 1944. An agreement was drawn up with the help of a British and an American officer who succeeded in entering the country and met the leaders of the three main organizations. This settled, for the time being, the military arrangements under which the guerilla warfare was to continue, and at its conclusion Colonel Sarafis of E.L.A.S. and Colonel Zervas of E.D.E.S. expressed the hope that future differences between them should be settled by arbitration.

There remained, however, a political problem. The guerillas, and in particular the E.A.M. (the political directive of E.L.A.S.), had for some time been demanding that they should send representatives to the Government in Cairo. While agreeing in principle to this, the then Prime Minister, M. Tsouderos, took the line that the guerillas must first put an end to their feuds. He did, however, begin some negotiations for a wider government—but too slowly and inconclusively for E.A.M. and the more lively of their sympathizers among the Greeks scattered in the Middle East. E.A.M. not only wanted to see a Government in Cairo completely free from what they regarded as the taint of Metaxism, but they tried to exact from the King a promise that he would not return to Greece until after a plebiscite had been taken to determine what kind of regime the people wanted. The King took the view that he should return to Greece at the first opportunity and that a plebiscite should be taken afterwards. He pledged himself to abide by the decision of his people as expressed in the plebiscite and elections. In December 1943 there was published a letter from the King to his premier in which he said: 'I shall examine anew the question of the date of my return to Greece.' This seemed to promise some concession.

Impatient at delays and what were perhaps inevitable difficulties, E.A.M. set up a 'Political Com-

mittee' in the mountains. News of this was received
at the end of March 1944. The Committee represented various parties in the E.A.M. organization
and was presided over by Colonel Bakirdzis, long
known as the 'Red Colonel'. He is a former Veni-
zelist revolutionary and was an opponent of the
Dictatorship.[1] While not claiming to be a rival
government it would appear that the Committee,
which immediately entered into relations with Tito
in Yugoslavia, assumed authority to speak for the
Greek people, or at least for the whole resistance
movement—an assumption that was clearly not
accepted by the Cairo Government.

DEMANDS FOR GOVERNMENT CHANGES. These
political demands of E.A.M. and the delay in meeting them, found sympathy among various groups in
the Greek fighting forces in Egypt—forces composed partly of Greeks from all over the world and
partly from Greeks who had escaped from the
mother country to fight with the Allies. A sit-down
strike broke out among the companies of several
Greek ships in the Middle East (who for three weeks
refused to obey orders or serve on convoy duty) and
in the First Greek Brigade (which was due to leave
for the Italian front almost immediately). The
mutineers, as indeed they were from the standpoint
of the Military Command (although the rebels dis-
owned this title) declared they would not renew their
service until the guerillas were represented in the
Government. The rebellion, which was a serious
handicap to allied operations, was successfully dealt
with by the Greek and British military authorities;

[1] Colonel Bakirdzis was later succeeded by Professor
Svolos.

but M. Tsouderos resigned in consequence and the King asked Colonel Venizelos (son of the former statesman) to form a Government. Colonel Venizelos was not able to do this and on 26 April 1944 the premiership was accepted by M. George Papandreou, leader of the Social Democratic Party, who had left Greece a few weeks previously and might therefore be expected to have special knowledge of conditions in the homeland, although he himself had not participated in the guerilla fighting.

M. Papandreou immediately proceeded to summon a Conference of representatives of the Greek resistance movement, and twenty-five delegates met with him in the Lebanon in May. All these put their signatures to a National Charter consisting of eight points. These may be summarized as follows:

(1) Reorganization of armed forces of Middle East under a national flag.
(2) Unification of all guerilla bands.
(3) Personal security and political liberty of Greek people to be established after the liberation.
(4) Arrangements to be made for the supply of food and medicines to Greece.
(5) Security, order and liberty to be the prelude to a free choice of government.
(6) Severe measures to be taken against quislings.
(7) The material needs of the people to be satisfied after liberation.
(8) Greek national claims to be met.

The Conference also passed a unanimous resolution to cooperate with the Prime Minister in re-uniting Greece by forming (a) a National Government, and (b) a National Army.

The Conference appeared to be a great success

and it left a general impression that unity was at last achieved. Unfortunately, however, differences developed once more between the E.A.M. and the Greek Government. Although the leaders of the E.A.M. and the representatives of its 'Political Committee' had concurred in the decisions of the Conference (including the condemnation of the mutineers), and despite the message which these delegates of the extreme left sent to Mr Churchill, thanking him for his interest in Greece and assuring him that they would do all in their power to achieve national unity, it would appear that when the decisions of the Conference were referred back to the E.A.M. group in the mountains, objections were raised. While other groups nominated their representations to the new Government of National Unity E.A.M. was silent. After a challenge, broadcast by M. Papandreou, E.A.M. sent telegrams to Cairo, making new conditions for its participation in the Government and demanding that its delegates in Cairo should return if these conditions were not fulfilled. Broadcasting to the nation at the beginning of July, M. Papandreou said that E.A.M. had demanded the increase of its representatives from four to seven (in a Cabinet of fifteen) and was resisting the incorporation of E.L.A.S. into a national army. The ministries which the E.A.M. demanded were key positions, including the Ministry of the Interior and the Under-Secretaryship for War. This amounted to giving E.A.M. the control of the Government and to this the Prime Minister was not prepared to agree. In August, however, the E.A.M. agreed to join the Government with five portfolios. In September the Government, anticipating the early liberation of Greece, moved to Naples.

Chapter IV

DAILY LIFE OF THE PEOPLE

In a previous chapter the geographical appearance of Greece was described, and in the following one the economic problem of wresting a livelihood from the country will be examined. This chapter gives a picture of the people, as they live against their background of mountain and sea, and as they work out their personal problems of finding food, clothing and recreation.

THE GREEK VILLAGE. Most of the people of Greece live in villages or small townships, and where these are near the sea they will often be found at some short distance from the coast, built on the slope or summit of a hill. This is explained partly by the necessity in earlier times to escape the depredations of the pirates who infested the Mediterranean and the adjoining seas, but who rarely ventured far inland. But it is also due to the still present fear of malaria. Swamps and marshes at the mouths of rivers, irrigation channels and even the puddles left by rain-storms are in Greece, as elsewhere, the natural breeding places of the malarial mosquito.

Most Greek towns and villages are of stone, and those houses which are built of earth (like the cob houses of Devon) are covered with white or pink wash which makes them stand out sharply against a background of green fields or cyprus trees. Every village has its central square with a few old trees

providing shade over a spring. On one side there is
usually the church, with the porch facing the square,
but the churchyard will probably be at some distance, outside the village. The town hall, the village
market and the chief café occupy the other sides of
the square, and on the seats outside the café the old
men sit and talk during the day and the women come
to fill their large earthenware pitchers from the
spring. At the end of the day, and especially on Sun-
days, the men come in from the fields and the square
becomes full of life.

Under the Turkish occupation all Greek villages
had a very closely knit communal organization, but
under the impact of Western influence this largely
broke down, although before the present war there
was talk of trying to recreate it by decentralizing administration. However, something of the old communal arrangements still persists. Many villages
have their own doctor, employed on a salaried basis,
to give both treatment and medicine to those who
fall ill. The grazing grounds are also communal
property, and at daybreak the whistle of the herds-
man means that cows, sheep and goats are going
out through the streets to the common pasture.

WORK ON THE LAND. Nearly all the men and
women of the village work on the land, and the
majority of them on their own holdings or with their
own animals. Those who have a mixed farm have
fewer anxieties than the specialized farmers. They
may have a few fields of wheat, a small olive grove
and a vineyard, and these will probably be scattered
in strips some distance apart, since each requires a
different soil. Livestock may consist of a mule, a

cow, a few sheep and goats. Other farmers grow a single specialized crop. In Thessaly, for instance, there are wheat farms, in the north of the Peloponnese, currant farms, and in Macedonia, tobacco plantations. For the wheat farmer there is no problem other than the weather, but those who grow currants or tobacco are also dependent on an insecure export trade—a problem that is dealt with in another chapter. When foreign buyers were ready and able to pay a good price for these export crops, the villages in the producing areas became prosperous. Debts were paid to shopkeepers and to money lenders; the brighter boys could be sent to a secondary school and all the children got better clothes. But there have been years in which great quantities of currants could not be sold even at a loss, and were either left to rot in warehouses or turned into methylated spirit. Then the usurer would foreclose on the little orchard which was perhaps the whole dowry of the wife, or on her few jewels, or on the vineyard itself and the dwelling of the family. Many independent small-holders were forced to become homeless, uprooted wage-earners, working for a pittance on other vineyards whose owners could put forward the reasonable excuse that next year they might be homeless themselves.

The currant grape requires a good deal of attention before it becomes the familiar currant: digging and fertilizing, sprinkling against phylloxera and other diseases and protection with waterproof coverings in case of sudden downpour. The small currant farmer who does not produce the minimum of the necessary food for his family has to incur a heavy debt at the local shop.

In addition, there is the weather: too little rain in the spring will dry up the vines. A Greek proverb says: 'Should March send two rains, and April one more, happy is the farmer who has sown much.' And in late July when the fruit is gathered and spread out to dry, a few days of uninterrupted sunshine, with dry, cold nights, are invaluable to the farmer. They usually come about, but if the heat has been excessive, and the accumulated vapours suddenly condense into a short torrential downpour, a year's toil and hopes and plans have been in vain. The same things are true of tobacco growing except that the rain must fall or abstain from falling at different times.

At a certain time in the twenties, so hard was Greece pressed that the State imposed a reduction in the areas cultivated with currants and tobacco. The peasants were heartbroken, for it meant changing their whole mode of life. The area sufficient to maintain a family by currants or tobacco is not nearly enough to produce the equivalent of wheat, olive-oil, vegetables and cattle fodder. The credits given to the peasants in compensation were soon spent; the peasant does not know how to make money 'bear', as the Greek word for interest says. And for those who had to uproot their ancient vines it was like losing live creatures.

The Greek State, despite errors of judgment and misguided measures, has always concerned itself with the problem of how to mitigate the risks of the single crop farmer. The Agricultural Bank, which was a State institution, was established to grant short- and long-term loans to producers at a low rate of interest. The Bank had its own expert assessors who visited the areas concerned and esti-

mated the probable yield; long-term loans were
granted for improvement of the soil and for agricultural machinery. Arrears have been also re-
peatedly reduced or remitted. The village co-
operatives, under the Bank's auspices, united the
farmers of a certain area, and mechanical ploughs,
threshing-machines and other necessary implements
were owned collectively and served all the small-
holdings in turn. Lastly, the Wheat Concentration
Scheme, put into operation a few years ago, tended
to encourage the cultivation of grain by equalizing
the price of imported and native cereals; it has
worked throughout very smoothly and efficiently.

THE SHEPHERDS.   In some parts of Greece another
kind of countryman is found, quite different from
the farmers with their settled homesteads. This is the
semi-nomadic shepherd. Many of these are Vlachs,
a people related to the Rumanians. They live on the
high Alps in the summer, under shelters made of
spruce and pine branches, and in the lowlands in the
winter. Their furniture consists mostly of strong,
elaborately carved and painted wooden boxes and
of woven blankets, rugs, covers, cushions and so on.
They possess a number of pack mules and horses in
addition to their thousands of sheep; their cattle are
less plentiful. They live mostly on their own produce, but in the winter they lay in stocks of rice, oil,
and other groceries. Their women are as expert
as the men in milking and in making cheese and
butter and tending the flocks. They set up their
rooms in the open air and weave their enduring
coloured fabrics, having spun the wool from spindles
hanging from their waist. One can often see cara-

vans of pack horses cross the streets of a provincial
town in the autumn, with the sun-burnt women and
the barefoot children running in front or behind, all
supremely indifferent to the sights offered by the
town. An old shepherd would formerly curse his son
because he had built himself a house. Theirs is a
traditional sort of culture, reduced to the essentials.
Their children used to go to schools rather fitfully
during the winter months only; but latterly the
Greek Government appointed teachers who would
follow them in their wanderings, teach in the summer under a roof of branches, and take their holidays
in the busy seasons of the shepherds.

THE PEOPLE OF THE ISLANDS. The Ionian islands
and Crete as well as Chios, Samos, Mytilene and
Euboea, are large and fertile enough to allow of a
mixed economy; but the smaller Aegean islands de-
pend mainly on the sea. Most of their inhabitants
are sailors and fishermen, and their life is a constant
struggle against the elements and the vagaries of
international trade. At all times the Greeks have
been among the most highly skilled and hardy sea-
farers of the world. Even under Turkish domination their ships, sailing under the Russian flag (a
concession forced upon the Sultan for the protection of his Orthodox subjects), had captured most of
the Middle East trade; from the innermost confines
of the Black Sea to the north of the Adriatic, and
from Aden and Alexandria to Marseilles or Cadiz,
Greek schooners and freighters carried all kinds of
merchandize. The tonnage and the value of the ships
furnished for the Greek War of Independence by the
diminutive islands of Spetsae, Hydra and Psara seem

fabulous. At the end of that struggle they had all been sunk, but the Greeks began again from the beginning with small steamers and cargo ships; they extended their voyages to all parts of the world, and it was not rare to see a faded Greek flag over a battered hull in Liverpool, Hamburg, Archangel or San Francisco. They were nearing the million ton mark when the last Great War broke out, and half of that tonnage was lost in fetching and carrying for the Allies. Later the tonnage rose to nearly two million tons, more than half of which has again been sunk in the present war.

The life of the sailors' families is one of protracted suspense relieved by short spells of home-coming and affluence. The Greek sailor is very faithful to his people at home and sends them every penny he can spare. The sailors' remittances, in fact, were one of the main props of the ever-precarious trade balance. But even so the women and children often have to rely on their own efforts, the few olive-trees and the little patch of a vineyard. The families of the fishermen have shorter spells to wait, but fishing yields proportionately less. For long periods there has been little planning and many fishing areas are depleted owing to catches in the wrong season and to the use of dynamite. Fishing tackle and machinery are also obsolete and refrigerators rare—so that much is wasted on the way. The Greek fishermen are a fine class of men: hard-working, abstemious, skilled in all kinds of work and used to the capricious ways of their seas.

THE WOMEN. Greek village women, whether the wives of peasants, sailors or fishermen, work very strenuously. In addition to their house-work and the rearing of a large family—it is considered a disgrace to have no children—they often work on the fields at the side of their husbands. Most of them know how to plough and dig, prune and sprinkle the vines, or harvest and winnow their grain. And their household work is much more than cooking, cleaning and mending. More often than not the bread is kneaded and baked at home, and when the ewes are shorn, the wool is given to the women who wash it in the stream, card and spin it, and then spread it out on the long woof, passing every thread through a knot of string on the upstanding frame.

During the long summer afternoons the women set up their weaving loom under the vine pergola in the courtyard; the big branches of ripening grapes sway overhead in the light breeze, children run in and out of the house shouting, the beans for the supper simmer in their onion and oil on the outdoor brazier, and the regular beat of the loom accompanies the women's low song. Hand weaving is strenuous work, but for women, used to walking long distances to and from the fields and to digging and loading the wheat, it is almost a relaxation, especially when they weave, not for the market, but for their own outfit. The girls begin preparing their bridal clothes, household linen, blankets and rugs, at a very early age. They store these things separately in strong wooden boxes, ornamented with paintings and carvings, and never use them before they are married. There is a story of a husband, who, being asked by his wife for money to buy some clothes, exclaimed in surprise: 'What? and we have not been married five years yet!'

RURAL INDUSTRIES. Every part of Greece has distinctive traditions in weaving, with characteristic patterns and colours. The districts round Parnassus are famous for their multi-coloured woollen blankets and rugs, Epirus for a sort of broadcloth and for saddle-rugs, southern Peloponnese for fine silk materials. In the years between the two wars, industrial production of woollen and silk fabrics increased very fast, and even made additional imports of raw silk necessary, though Greece produces silk of her own. But hand-weaving also increased. It became the fashion among wealthy classes to buy peasant rugs and to have their summer dresses made of fine hand-woven silk or cotton and their overcoats out of saddle-cloth. Nor was this tendency towards native products confined to clothes. Hand-made furniture in the style of the island houses, with elaborate wood-carving, as well as native pottery shared the vogue.

This sudden demand for things which had never before been reckoned as of much market value threatened the traditionally high standard of workmanship. The chance of easy gain encouraged the peasants to simplify their patterns and to use chemical dyes. On the other hand, there was some attempt by artists and antiquarians to enrich the native traditions by reviving some of the designs of ancient Greece. This was done in Crete, where an organization adapted genuine Minoan designs to the islands' particular style of weaving.

To Western minds life in a Greek village might well seem to be devoid of both amenities and entertainments. For instance, there is no electricity in the Greek countryside, and there seems little likelihood of it being introduced. Even where water-power could be utilized the need to import heavy plant would be a great strain on an economy where imports always tend to overbalance exports. Gas and coal fires are also hardly known, for Greece has no coal and wood has to suffice. According to some opinions the best way to make life easier for the country people would be to introduce communal improvements—for instance, village baths and washhouses. But it would be a mistake to think of the Greek peasants as depressed and weary people. Quite the contrary is true as their gallant resistance to the enemy has shown. Their houses, their way of life, have grown out of an age-long struggle with difficult conditions; and their intense interest in what is happening in the world and in their own country in particular, is born and bred in the national character. In earlier years there was a good deal of emigration to America, but many of the emigrants returned to their native village after enjoying a period of relative prosperity. This accounts for the fact that even in remote places in Greece an English-speaking villager will emerge to talk to the English or American traveller and act as an interpreter for the host of questions which his fellow countrymen will want to ask. The best hospitality that the village can provide will be lavished on the stranger.

RELIGIOUS FESTIVALS.   There are no entertainments, as the Western world understands them, in the villages; the peasant's home has no wireless set and the village no cinema. But local religious festivals provide for a break in the ordinary routine of hard work. They are usually preceded by an all-night vigil in and around a church or monastery and are associated with the local patron saint whose relics or ikon are often believed to have worked miracles.

On the evening before the festival the whole family sets out on foot, with the mule or donkey loaded with all the requisites for a protracted feast and for spending the night in the open air. The evening service is attended, and the most pious stay all night awake in the church. The ceremonial liturgy in the morning draws all villagers in their best clothes, including the children who are led to Communion. Later on begin the elaborate preparations for the midday meal. There are usually lambs roasted on the spit with eggs, cheese and lettuces, tomatoes or cucumbers. Large slices of yellow melon or green and red water-melon are handed round. One family may have brought a sweet pie made of nuts, butter and honey in a big baking dish, and offers a piece to every acquaintance. The entrails, liver and kidneys of the animals are woven together in a sort of plait which, roasted also on the spit, provide appetising tit-bits. Spirits and wine are passed from hand to hand. Hawkers offer less substantial sweets or gaudy wares. Then the music starts. There will be violinists who have learnt 'practically', as the Greek expression goes, that is, by ear, and other musicians play the mandolin, the guitar and the three-corded lyre. Finally the dance begins. A long row of people hold hands and follow each other's steps. The protagonist is in front and his skill and grace are followed with great attention by the experts among the onlookers. When enthusiasm reaches its peak, his admirers show their appreciation by placing a silver coin or a note on the violinist's forehead, and the violinist immediately redoubles his efforts. Meanwhile the elders sit on, watching and talking, and it is at these times that parents often arrange matches for their sons and daughters.

In addition to these local 'panegyria' there are other religious occasions—Christmas, the New Year, Easter and the days consecrated to the Blessed Virgin. The Easter ceremonies are the longest and most impressive. In Holy Week there is a general fast, everyone abstaining from meat, eggs, cheese and milk. On Good Friday the church bells toll all day and the people are dressed in mourning. Inside the church, where a plaintive chant goes on, there is the sacred pall, representing the bier of Christ. The young girls come in to lay flowers upon it and small children creep under the table on which the pall lies. An even stricter fast, which forbids even olive-oil, continues till dusk. Then the church fills and, after the appropriate service, the embroidered pall is carried out in procession, while the faithful follow bearing lighted yellow candles. The procession goes round the neighbourhood, sometimes quite far afield, while the priests at its head chant and the people who stand by the side of the road take off their hats and make the sign of the cross. Finally, the pall is returned to the church, where the service continues far into the night. On Saturday an air of expectancy and a bustle of preparation stirs every household. The men go about their business, or engage a little boy to carry home all they are going to buy—a whole lamb if they can afford it, as well as butter, cheese, onions, celery and eggs, lemons and oranges by the dozen. Tomorrow the lamb is to be roasted on the spit or in the oven. Meanwhile the women clean the whole house and bake a special kind of 'brioche'. The Easter eggs have been boiled hard and dyed red on Thursday. An hour before midnight every one goes to church. The churches are filled to capacity, and every year at this time the papers print long leaders on the imperative need of more church buildings. Thousands of people gather on the squares or other open places outside the churches, each one carrying a taper—white this time—and looking at the church windows. When these grow lighter and hundreds of little flames can be seen through their panes, people know that the moment is near. The priests and deacons in their heavy gold-embroidered vestments, the choir boys in their white surplices, carrying the banners and emblems of the church, emerge from the doors and take their places on a stand erected for the purpose. Amid the hushed silence of the thousands, the quavering voice of the oldest priest reads the passage of the Gospel which describes the pilgrimage of the women to the sepulchre and the answer of the Angel: 'He is not here, He is risen.' The candle flames dance up and down, the bells are rung at their loudest, fireworks illuminate the sky, the soldiers who have been holding their rifles reversed as at a funeral, present arms, friends and relatives kiss each other in gladness, while the choir repeats again and again: 'Christ is risen from the dead, vanquishing death by his dying and giving life to the entombed.' The tapers have all been lit from the central lamp at the altar, and those who manage to bring the flame home and keep it unquenched in an oil lamp for forty days are blessed in their homes; that is why, if a gust of wind extinguishes your candle on the way home, you approach anybody in the street and re-kindle your flame from his. 'Christ is risen', you say, 'Truly He is risen', the unknown friend answers.

Before the present war these ancient ceremonies happened, not only in isolated mountain villages, but everywhere in Greece. In Athens they were carried out with even greater splendour. The King and cabinet ministers, generals, admirals, higher civil servants and university professors all attended on both Good Friday and Saturday night. Under the warm moonlit sky, the Athenians become once more, as in their best days, a community.

THE TOWNS. Although Athens and Salonika and some of the other larger towns have taken on the general characteristics of all large towns in Europe and include extremes of wealth and poverty, the smaller towns have not greatly changed and social distinctions are not marked. The local magnates of a Greek provincial town are the wealthier farmers, the chief shopkeepers, the lawyers, doctors and town officials. There are no great landowners, for the large estates which once existed in Thessaly were broken up and the former tenants became proprietors. There is no country-squire tradition in Greece to give status to the landed proprietor, and ambitious men prefer the attractions of the larger towns.

The houses in Greek towns, especially in Athens and Salonika, reflect various influences. There is first the house, dating from Turkish times, whose life centres in its interior, with few windows on the ground floor, the upper storey jutting out into the street; it has a tiled roof and lovely gardens of which nothing is to be seen from the outside. Unfortunately many Athenian houses of this type, huddled round the Acropolis, have been demolished to make room for excavations which have not been very fruitful. The waste ground thus created an ugly gash in the face of Athens. Another style, which prevails also in many provincial towns, is the rectilinear, more or less box-like, house of two or three storeys with symmetrical windows on all floors, a flat roof and a balcony or two on the street. Such houses were considered characterless, but some achieved a sober harmony that was quite pleasing. They compare favourably with the flights of fancy of German-educated architects, who have added turrets, bastions, or Moroccan patios at random.

Athens also has its large modern blocks of flats, similar to those found all over the continent; they too often obstruct views which earlier generations had enjoyed. Yet another style, but a less common one, is the town house which is a replica of the island home—rectangular, with an interior white-washed courtyard and balconies overlooking this.

The interior of these houses are sometimes furnished with machine-made articles, but as has already been said, there was a growing fashion for things made by the village people, such as Skyros furniture chests that had been made to hold the dowry of a village bride, or rugs woven in Crete.

TRADITIONAL CULTURE.   The same mingling of old and new is found in Greek painting. The only genuine traditional painting of Greece is Byzantine and examples are to be found, unspoiled, in some Greek churches and monasteries. After the country achieved political independence this traditional art was neglected and Greek artists studied in Germany and Paris. Before the present war, however, there was an attempt to revive the Byzantine tradition and combine it with modern European developments.

But the best traditional culture of Greece, more striking than the country dances, is found in the folk-songs and this heritage of superb music is in danger of being lost. Composed in the old, non-tempered mode, these ancient tunes cannot be written down in our tempered scale and notation without distortion, and orchestration would ruin them. They can in fact, only be learnt and played by ear on fiddle or wood-wind and their survival depends now, as formerly, on one generation learning from another. The poetry of these songs, however, marks the beginning of modern Greek literature.

CHAPTER V

THE ECONOMIC STRUCTURE

Greece is a land of great contrasts and great variety.
A Mediterranean country on the fringe of the hot
African continent, it frequently comes in the winter
under the influence of the Asiatic high pressure belt
of climate. Two-thirds of the country is mountainous
but climatic extremes are tempered by a sea studded
with a hundred islands which surrounds the land on
three sides and penetrates deeply inland, forming
deep gulfs and innumerable bays and creeks. The
mountain chains cross each other in an inextricable
pattern. They isolate plain from plain or plain from
the sea; they tower steeply behind the flat coastal
strip cutting it off from the country behind; they
screen the valley or the lowland basin from the sun
and bar the rain here while letting it sweep inland
farther away.

The geographical position, the mountains and the
sea combine to create a great variety of soil, climatic
conditions, natural vegetation and crops.

COMMUNICATIONS.   In such a mountainous country
land communications are poor. Railways are few
and the road network is undeveloped. In the mountainous regions where only stony paths and mountain
tracks lead to the villages in the highlands, donkeys,
mules and mountain ponies are the only means of
transport. The deep gulfs, narrow straits and short
distance from island to island must in any case have
encouraged sea transport, which was further stimu-

lated by the fact that transport by land is so difficult and expensive.

Greece, like Norway, relies a great deal on coastal shipping. Before the war, apart from its ocean-going fleet, Greece had a fleet of eighty small coastal passenger and cargo ships, ranging from 100 to 1000 gross tons. Most of the passenger ships left Piraeus in the evening and called at the ports on the mainland or carried goods and passengers to and from the island. There were also 700 large sailing craft, most of them equipped with auxiliary engines, that plied busily between the various ports, loading or unloading lemons, grapes, melons, wine, tomatoes, onions and olive oil. One part of Piraeus is called the Lemon Harbour: it is used exclusively by sailing ships moored side by side and painted with bright colours.

These sailing or motor vessels of 30–400 tons were to Greece what lorries are to other countries. Since they can manœuvre easily even in small creeks and shallow waters they can carry goods from field to factory (oil and vineyard produce, for example) and to the shop or to the factory for secondary processing. They are especially valuable in a country where production is scattered and on a small scale and where seasonal production is so important and goods therefore require immediate dispatch.

There were also some smaller craft which were of great importance in local passenger transport, ferrying across narrow straits and gulfs from island to island and from island to mainland. In the gulf of Salonika, for instance, the suburban population living along the curving eastern shore, travelled directly to and from its work in small motor boats that departed from piers at regular intervals.

Even in the economically advanced countries of Western Europe, where distances have been considerably reduced by a well developed road, railway, waterway and air network and where the growth of industry tends to make local conditions uniform, human types differ remarkably in each region. This is still more striking in a country where local conditions change so much and where the communication network is undeveloped. Men and women vary and so do their habits, their beliefs and superstitions, their language, their way of building and decorating their houses. Although every Greek is of course, above all, Greek, yet when he is asked what the name of his fatherland is, he answers without hesitation, the Peloponnese or Macedonia, Thrace, Thessaly, or Epirus, or even such smaller localities as Laconia, Acarnania or Messenia, or his own island.

PRODUCTS AND POPULATION. A distribution map of the population of Greece would show large white patches of low density, mainly in the interior, the largest stretching from the Gramos mountains south of the Albanian border, to the Pindus range, which separates Thessaly from Epirus and to the barren limestone plateau of Attica. The bulk of the population is strung along the coast, and there are relatively dense clusters of rural population in the coastal strips that skirt the North, North-western and Western Peloponnese (a currant-growing area), the Messenia lowland shelf (a fruit- and vine-growing area), the small Argos plain (market gardening), the miniature plains of Amphissa (olives), Copais (cotton and cereals), Arta (citrus fruits), Volos (pears and apples), the Ionian and Aegean islands (olives and vines), the reclaimed fertile tracts of East Macedonia (cereals) and Thrace (tobacco and silk).

In Greece, as in other Balkan countries, the bulk of the population (about 60%) lives on the land. But only a small proportion of the total area in every Balkan country is cultivable and in Greece this proportion is the smallest—18% of the total area, while the proportion of the totally useless land is incomparably greater—55% of the total area. Many Greek mountains, especially in Southern Greece, are not covered with pastures or clad with timber-yielding forests like those of Yugoslavia, Rumania and Bulgaria, but are completely bare or grow only the short, stunted, sweet-smelling bushes called *maquis*, or trees whose wood is of indifferent industrial value. Only a few forests of the western mainland, Northern Greece and the Western Peloponnese, yield relatively good timber. Again, Greece, unlike her neighbours, is not fortunate in having continuous stretches of lowland producing a surplus of foodstuffs, which could be sent to other not self-sufficient regions or exported abroad. Only the small plains of Macedonia could send negligible quantities of cereals and livestock to the rest of Greece. All the Balkan countries have suffered from agricultural over-population, but in Greece the problem has been more acute than elsewhere. There were in Greece before the present war, 336 persons per square kilometre of cultivated ground as against 128 in Rumania, 140 in Bulgaria and 181 in Yugoslavia.

THE PEASANT ECONOMY. The Balkan countries are usually described as peasant countries. The peasant, unlike the farmer in Britain, who rents the land and the buildings on it from a landlord, owns his plot of land and everything on it, and in most cases takes part in the physical work in the fields. In the countries neighbouring on Greece, although the bulk of the population are poor peasants, most of the land is owned by large and medium peasants. Their holdings are of considerable size and they usually rely on hired labour for working them, confining their own work to the administration of their estates. Such holdings are capable of producing a surplus which is sold on the market, and it is from the market that the proprietors buy most of the goods which they need. In Greece this class of well-to-do peasants is less important and politically wields far less power. The typical Greek peasant is a small peasant, who seldom hires labour, and cultivates his own land (although the wealthier do employ seasonal workers at rush times for the harvest, gathering of grapes, for ploughing, digging of vines, pruning of olive trees and so on). If we calculate three to four hectares for each family as the minimum guaranteeing a subsistence level, it will be found that 94% of the Greek peasantry live below that level. The small peasant is self-sufficient not in the sense that he gets all that he needs from his holding, but in the sense that he covers the few requirements that he needs from what it produces. Thus he tries not to devote his land to one crop as the Rumanian and Yugoslavian peasants so often do, but, especially in Southern Greece, puts one strip under cereal, another under fodder. He may have a few olive trees and a small vineyard for his own wine, two or three almond and fig trees, and he may keep a few ewes and hens, a mule or two oxen and sometimes a pig.

There is also a class of what might be termed 'dwarf peasants', whose holding is too small and who can cover only a fraction of their needs from its produce. They may first complete some of the season's labour on their own holding (or leave it to their wives) and then go to work for a few months in the towns or in the fields of wealthier peasants; or, if they are islanders, they will sign on a ship for a few months and then return to their fields. Since they can find employment more easily at rush times, that is precisely when their own holding needs extra labour, they are compelled by circumstances to neglect their own land and perform the seasonal work either earlier or later than is required.

The peasant holding is not always compact. It is often parcelled up into strips, the one lying at some distance from the other. This results in wastage of labour and prevents the rational cultivation of the holding. Partly owing to ignorance but mainly because of his poverty, the typical Greek peasant employs primitive means of cultivation. Many peasants still harrow with a wooden harrow, do not use fertilizers, selected seeds or insecticides, and do not know how to prune their fruit trees. Modern agricultural machinery, such as tractors, reapers, binders and thrashers, is used only on a limited scale in Macedonia, Thrace and to a smaller extent in Thessaly.

EFFECT OF AUTARKY ON GREECE. Before the present war, 70% of the cultivated land in Greece was under grain and only 19% under those export crops (currants, tobacco and, to a smaller extent, cotton) for which the country is particularly suited. Although the climate, soil and prevailing system of small-holdings are unfavourable to grain production, and in fact the yield per hectare of wheat was the lowest in Europe, great efforts had been made during the years before the present war to double the production of wheat and other essential foodstuffs at the expense of what might be called the more natural products. This policy was forced on the country by the contraction of international trade and the prevailing tendency to autarky whereby, for instance, some countries planted tobacco despite unfavourable conditions. Currants, the most 'natural' product of Greece are a luxury foodstuff and therefore very dependent on the international market.

In spite of this drastic alteration in her economy, Greece had great difficulty in finding markets for her export crops and it was in this predicament that the country became tied up with the economy of Germany. Bilateral agreements were made whereby Germany bought up large quantities of Greek tobacco and other products and Greece in exchange received most of her requirements in coal, iron and steel, chemicals, machinery and manufactured goods. In the years 1929–38, Greek exports to Germany were nearly doubled and her imports from Germany were trebled.

The table on p. 76, which shows what proportion of the chief foodstuffs had to be imported before the war, illustrates clearly the dependence of Greece on imports.

The way to prosperity for Greece as her people see it, would be not to grow more foodstuffs, but to grow and export more of their special crops, fruits and vegetables. Then with the money obtained on the international market they would buy much larger quantities of foodstuffs than they could ever hope to grow on their own soil by extending the area under cereals and correspondingly reducing the area devoted to more natural products.

Foodstuff	Percentage of the consumption met through imports
Wheat	45
Other cereals	25
Dried vegetables	35
Rice	90
Sugar	100
Fish (fresh and tinned)	57
Meat	15

If Greece reduced the acreage under 'cash crops' to increase the acreage under cereals, she could grow somewhat larger quantities of foodstuffs at home, but she would be able to buy much smaller quantities of foodstuffs abroad and the standard of living would be ultimately brought down.

MINERAL RESOURCES. The chief mineral products of Greece are, in their order of importance, iron, pyrites, chrome, bauxite, lignite (brown coal), zinc, nickel, lead, antimony, and manganese. Greece has no hard coal or oil, although exploratory drilling in Northern Greece showed that the possibility of finding oil in the country cannot be excluded.

The contribution of minerals to the national income is not particularly high, but no systematic survey of the potential resources has ever been carried out and no serious attempt has been made to tap even the known sources or to process some of the exploited raw materials instead of exporting them abroad and importing the finished products. It is certain that, if the mineral resources of the country were fully exploited, they could make a much larger contribution to the national income. To take one instance only. There are vast quantities of bauxite (raw material of aluminium) in South-west and Central Greece, but only relatively negligible quantities have been mined and exported—mainly to Germany. Thus another step towards raising the standard of living in Greece would be the full exploitation of the country's mineral resources. This would react favourably not only on the working people directly concerned with mining but would also, if only to a small degree, relieve the pressure on land and therefore improve the standard of living of other sections of the population.

INDUSTRY. Because of her geographical position (on two important sea routes, one leading to the Black Sea and the other through the Suez to the Far East), the type of her production and the bareness of the soil, Greece has a relatively greater number of large and medium towns than any other Balkan country, and a much larger proportion of her population (40%) is employed in industry, including trade and shipping which occupy 18%.

Greek industry, which was born at the end of the nineteenth and in the early twentieth century, began to expand after the Balkan wars, when the supplying of the army, the doubling of the population and the acquisition of territory, which contained industries of some importance, fostered the growth of new industries and the expansion of old ones. The first Great War further stimulated the expansion of industry. Greek and foreign armies had to be supplied, despite shipping difficulties and the blockade; wealth accumulated during the war was invested in industry and a great reservoir of labour was created after the huge influx of refugees from Turkey in 1922.

In 1928, when the last census was taken, there were 182,000 industrial workers of both sexes. The majority of working people were men, except in the textile and tobacco industries, where women predominated. After the great crisis of the early thirties, when restrictions were imposed on imports and home production was effectively protected, Greek industry made another leap forward. Thus the volume of industrial production increased between 1928 and 1938 by 70% and the number of the working class was estimated before the war as between 350,000 and 400,000. Greek industry centred mainly in the Athens-Piraeus and Salonika regions which are more accessible and where there is a relatively large market and labour reservoir. It worked mainly on home-produced raw materials and imported semi-finished goods, but the small proportion (a fifth) of raw materials imported does not really reflect the dependence of Greek industry on imports. All fuel, liquid and solid, had to be imported and some raw materials used in small quantities were indispensable in the production of the finished goods. The cotton industry, for instance, used mainly Greek cotton, but it had to be blended with foreign cotton. Except for a tin-plate and small steel plant set up just before the outbreak of the present war, there is practically no heavy industry in Greece. The chief industries were: textiles, food industries, light engineering, building materials, leather, chemicals, paper and tobacco. Of these the most important on the basis of the number of people employed, the power used and the value of total production, were in 1930 (1) the food industry, concerned with the processing of products closely associated with agriculture (flour milling, olive oil and wine presses, canning, confectionery and edible pastes, alcohol, etc.), (2) textiles, and (3) the chemical industries. Although there were some larger textile, chemical, paper, cigarette and building-material factories employing a considerable number of workers and equipped with up-to-date machinery, most of the Greek factories (92% of the total number) were no more than small workshops employing from one to five men and using little or no power.

The development of Greek industrial production on a far greater scale is, in the Greek view, perfectly feasible and constitutes a further indispensable step in raising the standard of living of the Greek population. For not only would it improve the conditions of the working class which have been hitherto unsatisfactory but, by drawing people off the land and by increasing both the buying capacity of the working class and the home production of raw materials, it would react favourably on the conditions of the Greek peasants. Clearly the improvement of the peasant standard of living would in turn have favourable repercussions on the position of all other sections of the Greek population.

THE WORKERS' MOVEMENT. In the nineteenth and early twentieth centuries, the state of the working-class movement reflected the embryonic stage of development of Greek industry. Although there were a number of disconnected trade organizations and socialist groups in the larger towns of Athens, Piraeus, Syra, Volos, Kalame and Patras, the working class was organized, if at all, on the local craft basis. After the annexation of the New Provinces, 'Federation', the progressive organization of the Jewish working class of Salonika, exerted an important influence on the Greek working-class movement; it was also strengthened by the militant tobacco workers' organizations of Salonika and later of Kavalla, which have since constituted the backbone of the Greek labour movement.

At the outbreak of the 1914–18 war, the working-class movement was split into three factions, one supporting the Liberal party which advocated the entry of Greece into the war on the side of the Allies, the other supporting the royalist parties, which demanded that Greece should remain neutral, and an insignificant minority which claimed that the working class ought to follow an independent policy.

However, steps towards an independent development were taken in 1918 when the Socialist party of Greece, which included most of the local socialist groups and the General Confederation of Labour, was set up. In a few years many trades organized themselves on a national scale and in some cases related trades formed themselves into Federations which joined the General Confederation of Labour. The catastrophic post-war inflation, the explosive effects of the Russian Revolution and war weariness were responsible for a wave of strikes from 1920 to 1924. The working class, however, still lacked experience and was weak in its organization. In 1929 the Socialist party was split and the most important group changed its name to Workers' Communist Party and joined the Third International. The other socialist groups were never able to win any serious support.

In 1926 the Communist party withdrew from the General Confederation of Labour and formed, in 1929, the United Workers' Confederation. The crisis of 1932–4, which hit the working class severely, was marked by another wave of strikes. Great efforts were made to unite once more the working-class movement, but they were interrupted just as they were drawing to a successful conclusion by the dictatorship of General Metaxas, who abolished some of the unions and set up new ones organized on the Fascist model.

However, the unions managed to maintain skeleton organization underground and they are functioning to this day.

CHAPTER VI

THE EFFECTS OF ENEMY
OCCUPATION

REASONS FOR EXTREME SUFFERING. The German
Minister of National Economy has made the candid
admission that 'Greece has suffered more than any
other country from the effects of this war'. The
reasons for this extreme of hardship appear to be
five: (1) the structure of Greek economy and its dependence on foreign trade; (2) the sacrifices imposed
by six months of bitter fighting before foreign occupation; (3) the strategic position of the country in
the German plan of war; (4) the economic policy
pursued by the enemy in Greece—a policy that
differs from that adopted in other countries; (5) the
Greek people's stubborn refusal to look upon the
invaders as anything but enemies.

The economy of Greece and its dependence on
imported food have been described in a previous
chapter, and the table on p. 76 summarises this
dependence. The country could at the best only produce certain foods in sufficient quantity for the needs
of its people—olive oil and fats, milk, cheese, fruit
and fresh vegetables.

FIRST EFFECTS OF THE WAR. Under these conditions
the outbreak of war in 1939 and the destruction of
international trade which it entailed was bound to
have an adverse effect on the economy of Greece.
Total imports which exceeded 2,700,000 tons during
the pre-war period fell to 1,450,000 in 1940. Thus

even before actively participating in the war the Greeks experienced severe economic difficulties. This, however, was only a foretaste of what was to come, and it should not be forgotten that when Greece defied the Axis in the autumn of 1940, by taking up arms against Italy, she was embarking on a policy that was in every respect against her economic interests. As has already been explained, Greece was bound by close economic ties to Germany, Italy's senior partner in the war, and to imperil these was to court disaster. Moreover when Greece accepted the challenge of two Great Powers, her Allies were not in a position to give effective military or economic assistance. The result was that during the six long months of hard and unequal fighting the country had to draw heavily on its limited resources in order to meet the demands of the war. Practically all the means of transport were requisitioned for military purposes. Draught animals and tractors were similarly requisitioned on a large scale, and livestock had to be slaughtered for the needs of the army. This extensive requisitioning, coupled with the mobilization of the peasant population, reduced agricultural production by some 30%, and livestock by some 25%.

Industrial production also fell considerably owing to shortage of raw materials, fuel and manpower.

The result was a severe curtailment of consumption. The determination to resist was, however, so strong and universal that the population was ready to make every sacrifice and to bear hardships without complaint. It should also be noted that, while the country retained its political and economic independence and unity, these hardships, however great, left no section of the population completely unprovided for nor did they threaten the very existence of the nation.

The enemy occupation which followed brought to the country unprecedented privations and misery. A few months after the occupation famine was staring millions in the face and the extinction of a whole people appeared imminent. This deterioration of the situation was to some extent unavoidable and was due (*a*) to the total cessation of imports, and (*b*) to the sharp fall in agricultural production.

We have seen that under normal conditions the Greeks depended to a considerable degree on imports for the satisfaction of their needs in foodstuffs. Expressed in terms of calories this dependence amounted to one-third of the total consumption. After the occupation of the country, all imports ceased completely. The result was that a large section of the Greek population was left without alternative sources of supply. This section consisted mainly of the population of the urban centres, of the islands, of parts of the Peloponnese and of mountainous, arid districts, which had always depended on imports for their provisioning. The cessation of imports, which even in normal conditions would have severely affected the Greek food situation, occurred at a time when local production was undergoing a sharp and steady decline. As a result of the demands of the war effort, agricultural production fell by some 30% during the year 1940-1. Since the enemy occupation a further serious decline took place, due mainly to the following factors:

(a) The shortage of draught animals and of tractors. Of the 1000 tractors and 270,000 animals requisitioned for fighting, hardly 150 tractors and 80,000 animals were returned to agriculture.

(b) The shortage of feedingstuffs due to the fall of production.

(c) The lack of sufficient and suitable seed.

(d) The lack of fertilizers.

(e) Unfavourable weather conditions.

In addition to these factors, which would have reduced agricultural production under any circumstances, the conditions of insecurity created by the enemy occupation, the fear of requisitioning, the lack of means of transport, the financial dislocation and the arbitrary prices paid by the enemy for Greek products acted as a deterrent to the peasant and discouraged him from producing more than was absolutely necessary for his own subsistence.

The result of these unfavourable factors has been that the total quantities of foodstuffs produced during the period of enemy occupation have not on the whole exceeded 50% of pre-war totals. This, together with the cessation of imports, has meant that the total food supplies in the country since the enemy occupation have been below 40% of pre-war.

POLICY OF AXIS POWERS IN GREECE. An equitable distribution among the population of these supplies, however small, might have prevented a famine. This, however, was made impossible by the policy followed by the Axis Powers in Greece. The measures taken by the enemy have so completely disregarded the fundamental needs of the population, that it is no exaggeration to say that they correspond to a policy of virtual extermination.

One of the most pernicious measures adopted by the enemy in Greece has been the breaking up of the country into small, isolated regions between which practically no contact has been allowed. This measure has been responsible more than anything else for the disruption and dislocation of the economic life of the country.

Thus, Western and Central Macedonia, from which Southern Greece used to import a considerable part of her foodstuffs, became a separate region under German occupation from which practically all exports were forbidden. Crete and the Aegean islands were placed under a special regime which prohibited all economic transactions with other parts of Greece, even on behalf of the Greek civil authorities. The Cyclades islands were allowed to have economic contacts only with the Dodecanese. Similarly, the Epirus and the Ionian islands were completely isolated. A zone in the Evros department (in Thrace) under German occupation became a small independent region, deprived of any communication with the remaining parts of Greece.

Finally, the Germans allowed Bulgaria to incorporate two of the most fertile Greek provinces, Eastern Macedonia and Western Thrace; these, in the German and Bulgarian view, have ceased to be Greek territory. The Bulgarians have colonized this region under the name of 'the Aegean Province'. Any inhabitants of Bulgarian race automatically became Bulgarian, and Greeks and others (except Jews) could either accept Bulgarian nationality or leave the region before a prescribed date. Jews were deported.

The Jews have suffered in Greece the same indignities and cruelties that have been their lot elsewhere. They were obliged to register, to wear the Yellow Star of David, and to keep away from places of entertainment. The process of deporting them then began and they were sent off in truckloads to Poland. Only Jews of Turkish or Swedish nationality seem now to remain out of the large Jewish colony (50,000) in Salonika. Before the Italian collapse many Jews fled to the Italian zone of occupation in Athens, since the Italians did not impose the anti-Jewish restrictions. These, too, have since been rounded up.

No country subjected to such a splitting up of its territory could have escaped a complete dislocation of its economic life. In the case of a small country like Greece, with greatly diversified conditions and close interdependence between its various regions,[1] a country which was, moreover, occupied by three enemies with overlapping and often conflicting authority, such a measure could not fail to bring about complete chaos and disintegration. This measure was not dictated solely by military considerations. It was also found an effective means of exercising control over local supplies. This is borne out by the fact that prohibitions over the movement of commodities applied not only between the various isolated regions described above, but also within

[1] The Peloponnese and the islands produce mainly olive oil, fruits and vegetables, the centre and north mainly cereals, meat and dairy products. As a result of the measures described above, olive oil, which was desperately needed in Central and Northern Greece, and which was available in the islands in adequate quantities, was retained by the enemy in the centres of production and could make no contribution to the feeding of the population on the mainland.

regions. No goods could be transported from rural to urban centres without special licenses from the occupying authorities who saw to it that their own needs were met first.

If to this control over supplies be added the complete control over all means of transport, the picture that emerges is one of a real stranglehold exercised on the Greek economy. Means of transport had always been inadequate in Greece. During the period of active warfare very heavy losses were sustained, with respect both to road transport and to coastal shipping, on which over half the inland transportation depended. Practically all coastal vessels were sunk by enemy action during the war. The few vessels which were left at the time of the occupation of the country were immediately requisitioned. Similarly all serviceable road vehicles were taken over by the occupying authorities, while the railway system was almost exclusively reserved for the armies of occupation. A few old lorries and some small sailing vessels were all that was left for the needs of the civilian population. The result was that, even when supplies were available, they could not be moved where they were needed.

The policy described in the preceding paragraphs has enabled the enemy to lay hands on a considerable proportion of the tragically small quantities of local products available. These were used for the maintenance not only of the armies of occupation, in the strict sense, that is for the forces needed to police the country, but also for the much larger forces concentrated in Greece and intended for the Mediterranean theatre of war, as well as for troops recuperating from the Eastern Front. Moreover, the local products thus directed to the needs of these forces were supplemented by extensive slaughtering of live-stock. In addition, considerable quantities of Greek products were exported from the country.

In order to carry out this policy of spoliation, large sums of money were exacted from the Central Bank. They were used not only for the buying up of Greek products, but also for the construction of vast works of fortification required in order to make Greece the southern sector of the European fortress. Up to October 1943 the amounts thus obtained by the occupying authorities exceeded 1,000,000 million drachmae.

FINANCIAL DISLOCATION. When this figure is com-pared with a pre-war national income of 60,000 million drachmae, it is obvious that such a colossal sum could not be injected in the Greek economic system without creating conditions of runaway inflation. In fact, monetary inflation in Greece is on a scale exceeding anything that has been experienced in other countries in this war. The monetary circula-tion increased from 20,000 million drachmae at the time of the enemy occupation to 1,800,000 millions in October 1943. The general cost of living in the capital had increased 300 times up to October 1943, while the prices of foodstuffs on the Athens market had risen 1000 times.

Wages and salaries, on the other hand, had in-creased only 100–200 times by October 1943, while other incomes failed to catch up with the rise in prices even to that extent. At the same time, a small number of people have been able to enrich them-selves on the black market by taking advantage of the acute needs of their fellow citizens. Often black-market activities have been a combined operation between these unscrupulous persons and members of the occupying forces. An even smaller number of people have derived substantial advantages from collaborating with the enemy. The considerable purchasing power in the hands of these people will raise serious problems and will require stringent measures at an early date, if they are to be prevented from becoming the 'new rich' of to-morrow and from exercising economic power in the country.

Another phenomenon which completes the picture of economic dislocation is the disparity of prices in the various regions of the country. Prices in the urban countries are often ten times higher than in the centres of production. The whole financial and monetary structure of the country has been destroyed almost beyond repair.

In addition, the disruption which has taken place has resulted in widespread unemployment. With the exception of the activity created by the needs of the occupying authorities, economic stagnation is everywhere and is depriving large sections of the population of the means of earning an income. The lack of fuel and of raw materials has brought industry to a standstill. It is estimated that industrial output does not exceed 10–15% of pre-war and consists exclusively of goods produced on behalf of the occupying authorities. The lack of employment has driven some thousands of Greeks to accept the German offers of work in Germany. How many have gone it is impossible to say. Others have been forced to work for the Germans in Greece. After a Civil Mobilization Decree in February 1943, there were demonstrations in Athens and a general strike as a result of which the decree was withdrawn. Although it was promulgated again and the age limit in January 1944 raised to 65, it only seems to have been applied in a limited way in certain localities and for special purposes. In Crete, for instance, persons between 16 and 60 years of age are compelled to work for 10 days each month on road construction.

REASONS FOR AXIS POLICY.   Instead of recognizing that no material contribution could be expected from such a country without endangering the very existence of its people, the enemy followed the policy of systematic spoliation described above with a callousness which appears exceptional even by Axis standards.

This exceptional harshness of Axis policy in Greece may be attributed to two factors:

(1) Owing to the limited resources of the country and to the fact that Greece was not situated in the proximity of the Axis centres of production, the rational exploitation of the Greek economy presented small advantages to the enemy. While in most of the other occupied countries Germany found it profitable to maintain their economic and financial structure and ensure minimum rations to the working population, in the case of Greece the policy followed had only one object in view, namely to obtain from the country whatever was available or was somehow being produced. The methods used for carrying out this policy of easy and irresponsible spoliation have not only created chaos and disinte-

gration but their net result will be the permanent impoverishment of the country. Livestock provides a typical example. In some parts of occupied Europe bordering upon the Reich, the numbers have even been maintained in order that the Germans might obtain meat and dairy products for their own military and civilian needs. In the case of Greece, on the other hand, the cattle have been virtually exterminated. The decline which has taken place is estimated at 65 % of the pre-war figure.

The result is that Greece has been not only exploited but also ruined and will for a long time be unable to meet her needs from her own resources.

(2) The active resistance offered to the Axis before and during the occupation, which interfered considerably with enemy plans, as well as the hostile attitude maintained throughout by the Greek population, have been strongly resented by the enemy who felt that the miseries and privations endured by the Greek people were the inevitable and just consequence of their 'senseless' attitude in this war.

It is often believed that Germany treats friend and foe with equal ruthlessness. This, however, does not correspond to the facts. Hungary, Rumania, Bulgaria and the other countries who sided with Germany have on the whole been treated with consideration, and have derived certain economic advantages from their collaboration with Germany. It is also a fact that the Germans have not only discriminated between friend and foe: even as between their enemies the treatment meted out is in direct relation to the degree of hostility encountered.

The consequences of the measures adopted by the enemy in Greece could not be other than they have been: a whole population was threatened with extinction. The reduced local supplies could be stretched to meet the needs of about 3,000,000 people, consisting of the producers of food and of persons who could obtain foodstuffs in exchange for their goods and services. For the remaining population, however, the problem of obtaining the means of subsistence could not be solved without outside assistance.

FAMINE. During the period August 1941–April 1942, conditions of actual famine set in in Athens (1,200,000 population). Official distributions did not provide more than 350 calories per day on the average. A watery bean soup was being distributed to thousands of starving citizens in communal feeding centres and was providing another 140 calories. Erratic and inadequate distributions of low-quality bread and some vegetables and fruits obtainable on the market completed the food supplies available to the vast majority of the population. On the average the population did not obtain more than 600–800 calories[1] per head per day from all these sources.

Deaths from starvation assumed terrifying proportions and an alarming rise in morbidity took place. Conditions were even worse in the islands, while in urban centres other than the capital and in mountainous districts conditions, although less acute, were steadily deteriorating. In the early

[1] 2000 odd is generally regarded as the minimum number of calories for bare subsistence. For an adequate diet it is 2600.

months of 1942 it was generally recognized that, unless relief were to be forthcoming from outside, Greece would soon be transformed into a vast cemetery.

RELIEF MEASURES.   A partial raising of the Allied blockade was decided upon in the spring of 1942 and since then regular shipments of 15,000 tons of wheat, a gift of the Canadian Government, have been dispatched to Greece, to which were added later 3000 tons of dried vegetables and 100 tons of powdered milk supplied by the U.S.A. Government.

The distribution of these foodstuffs was entrusted to a Swedish Red Cross Commission. Stringent conditions were imposed for preventing any of these foodstuffs from benefiting the enemy. The Commission was even able to negotiate an agreement with the occupying authorities whereby the latter undertook to provide compensation for the local foodstuffs consumed by them or exported. This compensation, it is true, was expressed in terms of calories, which meant that the occupying powers were able to discharge their obligations under the agreement by importing a few thousand tons of sugar and dried beans in exchange for valuable local produce consumed by them. The scheme, however, was a vast improvement on the policy of ruthless and callous exploitation followed during the first two years of the enemy occupation. This partial reversal of policy was not only evidence that the enemy himself recognized that he had gone too far, it was also the result of the sharp fall in agricultural production, which made it increasingly difficult for the enemy to lay hands on any considerable quantities of local supplies.

The wheat placed at the disposal of the Relief Commission has enabled it to ensure a bread ration of 150–200 grammes per day (corresponding to 400–500 calories) to approximately 3,000,000 people. Of these, 2,000,000 people, representing mainly the population of the larger urban centres, receive in addition other relief foodstuffs (dried vegetables such as beans and peas and cereal products) which provide somewhat less than 300 calories per day. Thus, relief imports secure 400–500 calories per head per day to 1,000,000 persons and some 750 calories to another 2,000,000 persons.

The calories obtained by the majority of this section of the population from other sources, including enemy supplies, do not seem to exceed 300 calories per head per day. The gratitude of the Greek people to the Allied and Neutral Governments which have come to their assistance is deep and sincere. There is no doubt that the relief granted to Greece has prevented the extermination of nearly half its population, which would have been inevitable otherwise. It has not, however, prevented the grave physical exhaustion of the population, as can be inferred from the figures quoted above of the average calories supplied.

Not only is the calorie intake tragically inadequate, but it is also almost exclusively supplied from cereals and dried vegetables. The lack of animal protein has been one of the most serious deficiencies in the diet of the Greek population for the last three years, and the Relief Commission has reported a great number of cases of œdema among the population caused by this deficiency. The lack of fats is equally conspicuous.

RESULTS OF MALNUTRITION. This serious and prolonged malnutrition has resulted not merely in the lowering of the physical resistance and vitality of the Greek population, but also in the appearance of a great number of deficiency diseases among vast sections of the population.[1] In addition to severe conjunctivitis, sometimes leading to blindness, trachoma, which was widespread in Greece even before the war, has increased alarmingly. The Relief Commission has reported that one-third of the children of the Piraeus are affected with this disease. Tuberculosis has always been one of the major health problems in Greece. It was estimated that there were approximately 150,000 cases during the pre-war period and that deaths from tuberculosis exceeded 20 per 10,000 inhabitants. The conditions under which the Greek population has been living during the last three years have been particularly favourable to the further spread of this disease. As it was to be expected, tuberculosis has assumed terrifying proportions, particularly among the younger generation (it is estimated that there are over 500,000 cases at present).

Malaria has always been one of the chief scourges among the various diseases in the country. Greece was considered the most malarial country in Europe. Before 1930 there were 9·14 deaths from malaria per 10,000 inhabitants in Greece, as compared with 0·70 in Italy, 1·58 in Bulgaria and 0·29 in Spain. Since 1930, as a result of a vigorous anti-malaria campaign, deaths had been reduced to 5·5 per 10,000. No major area in Greece was free from the disease, but

---

[1] Osteomalaria is prevalent, as well as hunger œdema, pellagra and other deprivation diseases.

the rural communities suffered most (Macedonia, Thrace, Epirus and Thessaly were the regions most severely affected). It has been conservatively estimated that there were 1,000,000–2,000,000 cases during the pre-war period. 30–40 tons of quinine were imported annually of which 10% approximately was distributed free to the population. As a result of the lack of anti-malarial drugs, of the abandonment of the anti-malaria campaign and of the severe malnutrition of the population, malaria has now assumed appalling proportions and has spread to regions, such as the capital, where its prevalence had been small before the war.

Owing to lack of soap, fuel and the most elementary facilities for washing, scabies is universal. The children have suffered most from the conditions prevailing in the country. The Relief Commission has classified nearly half the child population of the capital in the category of those suffering from severe undernourishment and requiring special supervision. It seems that conditions are even worse in some of the provinces.

REPRISALS. Another factor has increasingly operated to extend the privation and misery prevailing in the country to those sections of the population which had hitherto been more or less self-supporting and had escaped the worst sufferings experienced by the people not themselves occupied in food-production. This is the system of reprisals resorted to by the enemy in retaliation for German soldiers killed and for acts of sabotage.

These reprisals take the form of burning whole villages, destroying or seizing the crops, shooting the peasants or driving them to the mountains. We know that the reprisals resorted to by the Italians alone before their surrender are likely to have affected some 100,000 peasants. Since the Italian surrender the Germans, who from the first took a firm revenge, notably in Crete, for any act directed against their troops, have been carrying out reprisals on an increasing scale. Special Commissions, under the auspices of the Red Cross and with facilities given by the Germans, investigated conditions on the spot in four regions and found, that up to December 1943 there had been 350,000 victims of reprisals. Later it was reported that the number had been doubled and was growing daily. According to reports in *The Times* of 26 and 27 January 1944, '1600 villages have been completely destroyed and nearly 2,000,000 peasants who have been made homeless are wandering in the mountains and starving'. The Relief Commission has tried to bring assistance to these unfortunate persons and relief shipments were considerably increased early in 1944. At the end of 1943 it became known that the puppet Prime Minister, M. Ralles, was organizing 'Security Battalions' to assist the Germans in dealing with the guerillas and that these battalions were terrorizing the people throughout the country. The Government in Cairo immediately ordered all Greeks thus recruited to desert by 3 January 1944 on pain of being black-listed for treachery. The result is not known, but it is clear that the formation of the battalions was furiously resisted in some parts, notably in Crete.

THE ATTITUDE OF THE PEOPLE. The Greek people have borne their trials with fortitude and dignity and have won the admiration of the foreign missions which are working among them. The following quotation is from the publication *The International Red Cross Committee in Geneva* 1863–1943 (p. 76):

One thing which has aroused wonder and admiration in all who have worked among this famine-stricken population must be mentioned here, and that is their extraordinary dignity in suffering, their patient endurance and the unfailing gratitude and docility with which they have accepted every measure judged necessary by those whom they know are trying to help them.

They have maintained their attitude of uncompromising defiance to the invaders and have not attempted to better their lot by showing the subservience which the enemy expected from a defeated and exhausted population. In this, it should be said, they have been supported by the leaders of the Orthodox Church. Most of the Metropolitans (Archbishops) have refused any collaboration with the Germans and many have suffered in consequence —including a large number who appear to have been sent to a concentration camp for refusing to preach anti-Jewish sermons. The Metropolitan of Kozani went to the mountains to join the guerillas. In Athens the Archbishop organized a system of soup-kitchens with branches all over the country, and this has been one of the most successful pieces of relief work.

NOTE ON LOCAL ADMINISTRATION IN GREECE

Under foreign occupation a country will usually keep much of its system of local administration intact. The following details on local authorities and local officials may therefore be useful to any Allied soldier or relief worker serving in Greece during an intermediary period.

Greece is divided into the following administrative areas:

1. Governments-General (Γενικός Διοικητής).
2. Prefectures (Νομός).
3. Provinces ('Επαρχιά).
4. Boroughs (Δῆμος).
5. Parishes (Κοινότης).

1. *Governments-General.* There are four of these areas: Macedonia, Epirus, Thrace, Crete. Each of these is under a Governor-General who ranks as a Minister of State and may attend Cabinet meetings. The Governor-General has absolute authority over his area except in military, naval and juridical matters.

2. *Prefectures.* The Prefects (Νομάρχης) function in those parts of Greece which are not under Governors-General, i.e. in Central Greece, Thessaly, the Peleponnese and the islands (except Crete). There are twenty-five prefectures altogether. Although not invested with as much authority as a Governor-General, the Prefect represents the

Government within the area in his charge. He is appointed by the Government and directly responsible to the Minister of the Interior. His chief duties may be summarized as follows:

- (i) To see that laws and government instructions are carried out.
- (ii) To supervise lower officials, e.g. subprefects, mayors, presidents of Parish Councils.
- (iii) To pass on complaints and requests to the Government.
- (iv) To issue prefectoral orders, within the prescribed limits of his powers.

Most of the larger islands are in charge of a Prefect. Smaller ones are usually under a Subprefect.

3. *Provinces or Sub-prefectures.* The Prefectures are divided into Provinces or Sub-prefectures, each under a Sub-prefect. These divisions, however, are relatively unimportant. The Sub-prefect merely acts for the Prefect and each Sub-prefecture is divided into town and county areas—boroughs and parishes (see below). These are important units of local self government.

4. *Boroughs.* A town of over 10,000 persons can claim the right to be made a Borough. In this case there is a Municipal Council (elected by all males who are parliamentary electors and by all women over thirty who can read and write) and a Mayor (Δήμαρχος), chosen by the Municipal Council. Aldermen, who will number eighteen or twenty-four according to the size of the Borough, are also elected and there are also three or four assistants.

It should further be noted that the Municipal

Council chooses three or five of its members (according to the size of the Council) to form a Municipal Committee (Δημοτική Ἐπιτροπή). Its duties may be summarized thus: (*a*) to supervise the affairs of the Borough, (*b*) to examine the budget, (*c*) to contract municipal loans, (*d*) to supervise auctions, (*e*) to approve public works or purchase of goods up to a prescribed limit, (*f*) to issue summonses.

The Mayor is not necessarily a member of the Municipal Committee. If he is chosen as a member, then *ex-officio* he is its chairman. Otherwise the senior member presides.

5. *The Parishes*. The Parish, in civil administration, covers the same area as the church Parish, but ecclesiastical and civil affairs are entirely separate in Greece, as in Britain.

The Parish Council is elected every four years and is the recognized authority in a village and the adjoining district. Its duties are not defined by law, but among other matters they cover the following: parish property, parish loans, appointment of parish employees, improvements and constructions in the Parish, the budget for parish welfare.

The Parish Council elects elders and these nominate one of themselves to be President. The President of the Parish (Πρόεδρος τῆς Κοινότητος) will be found to be the leading man in every village and the village's acknowledged representative.

HEALTH SERVICES

Doctors in Greece will, in most cases, be found to be very highly qualified. The medical Faculty of Athens University has an excellent reputation and the normal medical course covers seven years. Apart from this, most Greek doctors of standing before the war had an extended training in some foreign country.

There are three main departments in the State Medical Service:

(i) Department for Malarial Diseases.

(ii) Department for Social Hygiene. (This covers maternity and child welfare services.)

(iii) Department of Medical Assistance. (This supervises medical and pharmaceutical services for the poor and all medical and pharmaceutical establishments.)

The State Medical Service appoints officials in all the Greek prefectures. Besides this Central Health Service, municipal and parish authorities each have their own district doctors paid by these authorities. Small villages have no resident doctor. Every doctor in Greece offers free consultation to the poor once or twice a week, and it is a common sight to see sick people transported on mules to the nearest doctor on his 'free' day. Medicines can be had free on the production of a permit from the Ministry of Social Welfare.

Voluntary contributions and bequests combine with public money to provide for the care of the sick in Greece as they do in Britain. Hospitals are maintained in this way and provide treatment without charge for those who cannot afford to pay. The Patriotic League, a voluntary organization which receives State grants, provides a variety of health services, including convalescent homes, tuberculosis clinics and treatment for children.

The Greek Red Cross is very well organized and apart from the usual functions it maintains a training school for hospital nurses. The training which lasts four years is on the English model.

There is a State Midwifery Service for which the training is a three years' course.

INDEX